The Ridiculously Simple Guide to Numbers for Mac

Scott La Counte

RIDICULOUSLY
SIMPLE BOOKS

ANAHEIM, CALIFORNIA

www.RidiculouslySimpleBooks.com

Table of Contents

Disclaimer*: Please note, while every effort has been made to ensure accuracy, this book is not endorsed by Apple, Inc. and should be considered unofficial.*

INTRODUCTION

Microsoft Excel *used* to rule them all. It didn't matter what computer or operating system you had—if you needed to create a spreadsheet, you used Excel.

Times have changed! Today, there are many spreadsheet solutions out there. Some, like Google Sheets, are pretty barebones; and others, like Excel, feel at times feature creep—there are just so many options, it's easy to get lost. If you use a Mac, iPad, or iPhone, then you have a third option that's growing in popularity: Numbers.

In addition to being simple, yet visually stunning, Numbers comes free with Apple devices. What's even better is it's pretty easy to get started, even with limited knowledge of the software.

If you really want to get the most out of it, then this guide will help. It will show you the ropes—including how to do all those things you are used to doing in Microsoft Excel - and help you with some of the features you may not even know about.

Ready to get started? Let's go!

[1] THE BASICS

This chapter will cover:

- How to get Numbers
- Opening your first document
- Numbers crash course
- Formatting text
- Layouts and styles

HOW TO GET NUMBERS

Depending on how you acquired your Mac, you may or may not have Numbers already. Getting it is easy. And even better: getting it is free! (You can see if you have it by going into the Launchpad from the dock and searching for Numbers).

There's one catch: not all Macs are supported. But most are. MacOS 10.14 is required to run Numbers, which means you must have one of the following computers:

- MacBook: Early 2015 or newer
- MacBook Air: Mid 2012 or newer
- MacBook Pro: Mid 2012 or newer
- Mac Mini: Late 2012 or newer
- iMac: Late 2012 or newer
- iMac Pro
- Mac Pro: Late 2013 or newer; Mid 2010 or Mid 2012 models require a Metal-capable GPU

As long as you have one of those, then you can go to the App Store (it's in your Launchpad). Numbers is a digital download only—you cannot obtain a physical copy of it. The download is a few hundred MB.

From there, type in Numbers in the search bar, and hit the return key.

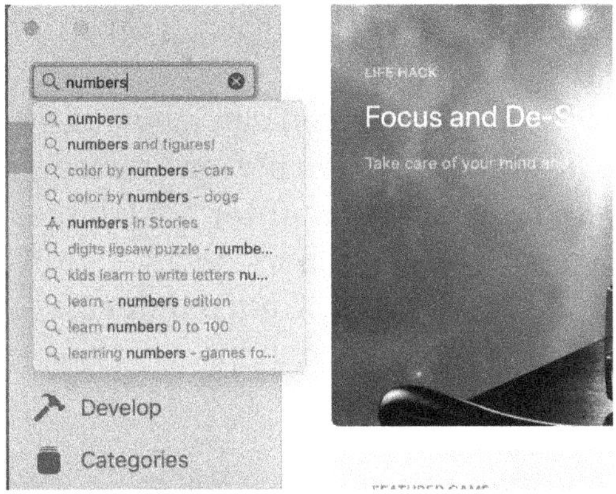

If you have it, the return result will have an Open button; if you don't have it, the result will show a Get button. When you click Get, you'll be prompted to put in your Apple ID and password; if you don't have an Apple ID, then follow the onscreen instructions to get one (this is free).

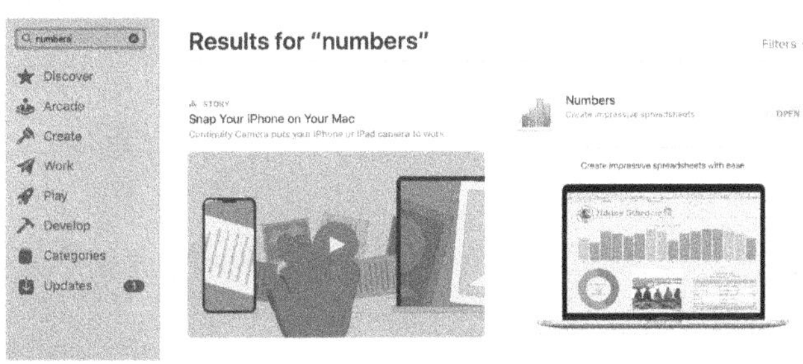

Running Numbers for the First Time

When you first open Numbers, you'll be asked if you want to use iCloud. I recommend you do; this makes it easy to save and open documents across all devices—if you are writing a document on your phone, for instance, you can open that document and continue working on it from your tablet—it's all very seamless and doesn't require anything extra on your part once it's set up.

If you set up iCloud, you can even access and type documents right in your browser—there's nothing else to install on your computer, which means "technically" you could use Numbers on a Windows computer or even a Chromebook or Android device—I'll show you how at the end of this chapter.

The Numbers Crash Course

The first time you use Numbers, you'll get a brief tutorial. You can either watch it or skip it.

Each time you open Numbers, you'll be greeted with a directory box that asks you if you want to open an existing document or if you want to create a new one. We'll be working off a new document in this chapter, so click "New Document" in the lower left corner.

The next box you'll see is all the available templates you can use. A template is a premade document that you can add text into. For example, if you want to create a calendar, you can use the calendar Template, and you will keep the formatting but type over the text that's there with the text that matches what you want. Templates are listed under categories.

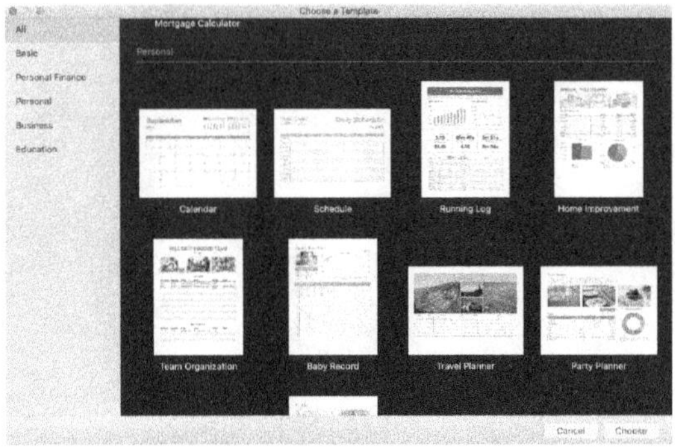

You'll probably notice something quite unique about some of these templates: they don't look like spreadsheets. Like everything Apple, they put a lot of detail into making things look beautiful. Yes you can do your old fashioned spreadsheet here, but you can do so much more.

If you don't want to start with a template, then click on the first option (which says Blank).

First time users of Numbers are often a little disappointed the first time they use Numbers; if you've Excel, then you have ribbons and menus and options everywhere! Numbers looks pretty bare next to that.

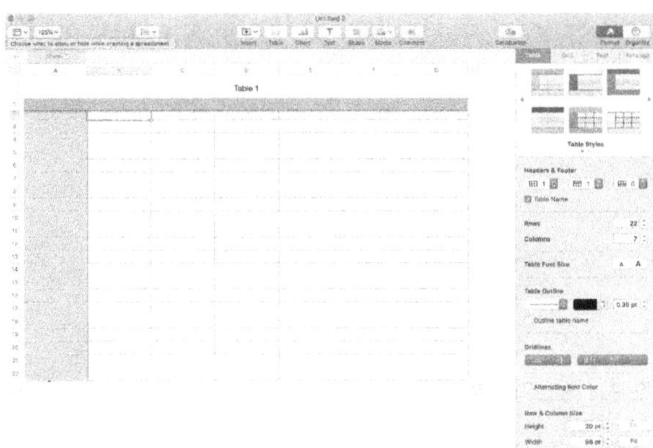

Don't worry—looks can be deceiving; there are plenty of options when you know how to find them, and I'll show you each of them in this book. If you need reassurance, look at those Templates again!

If you feel overwhelmed already because there are options, you can hide that side panel by clicking on the Format button in the upper right corner.

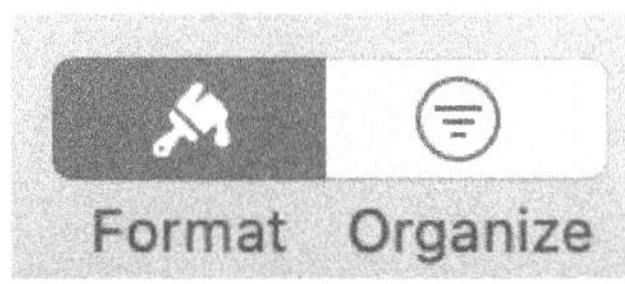

Now that you have a blank screen, let's go over the very basics of Numbers (you can click the Format button again to get the side panel back).

SELECT

To select a single a cell, move your mouse over it and click once.

SELECT INSIDE

To select inside a cell, click the cell and click twice.

SELECT OPTIONS

Now that you have the text selected, what do you do? If you click with two fingers on your trackpad or mouse, then the options box comes up. We'll go over what these options are as we continue the book.

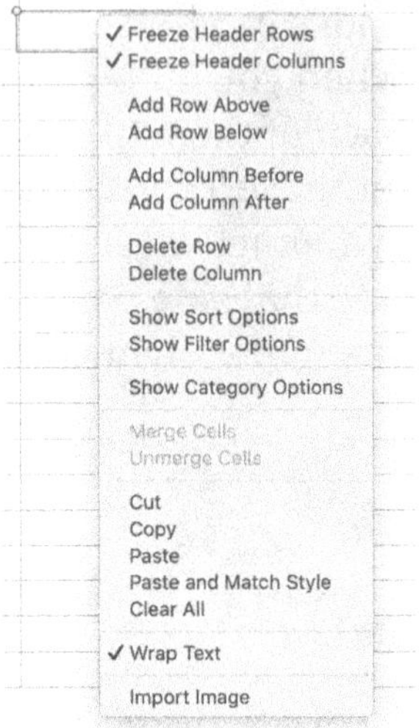

Cut, Copy and Paste

To copy and paste words (and images, tables and charts) quicker, you can use keyboard shortcuts.

Selecting content and hitting COMMAND + C will copy it.

Selecting content and hitting COMMAND + X will cut it.

And hitting COMMAND + V will copy the content anywhere you want it in the document.

Remember, if you click a cell and do this command, then you are copying the cell; if you only want the content in the cell (not the cell style, for example) then double click and highlight the content.

Find and Replace

Find and Replace is a handy little feature in Numbers (especially in large spreadsheets) that allows you to replace your selection with alternatives.

Let's say you just created a 1,000 line spreadsheet full of random names. But once you are done, you realize you need to spell one of the names (Sara) as Sarah. It can be done in seconds!

Go to edit from your menu bar, and select Find > Find.

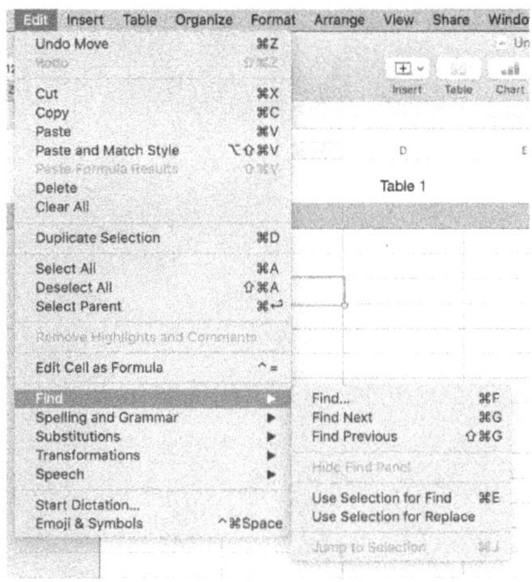

From here you can find all the uses of the word you want to find, but you can also click the down arrow on the left side and select Find & Replace. This lets you search for a word (top line) and replace the word once it finds it (bottom line). When you have both the find and replace word added, then you can click Replace & Find.

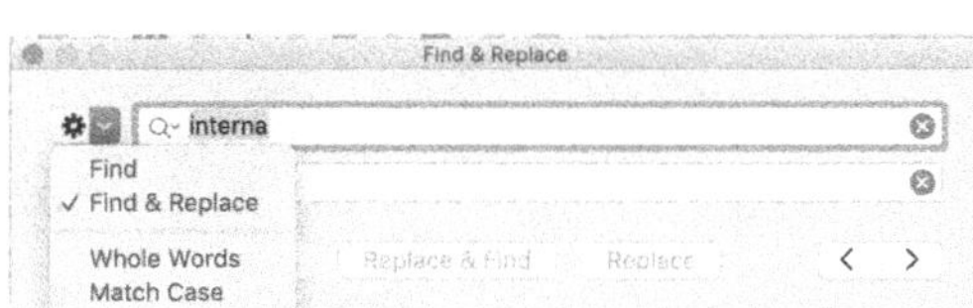

Define

Numbers has a handy little dictionary built in. You can select any word, tap the trackpad twice to bring up the options menu, and tap Look Up to see the definition of any word. Remember you need to select the word and not the cell.

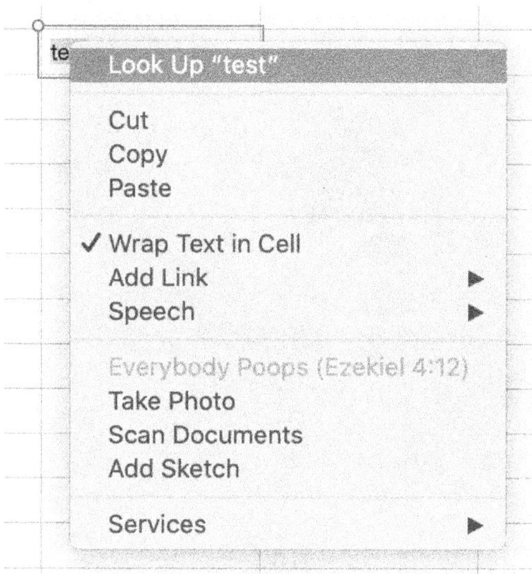

The dictionary will give you multiple definitions (and a thesaurus); even more, you can select options at the bottom to see movies related to the word, Siri Knowledge (which is encyclopedic information), apps related to it, and more!

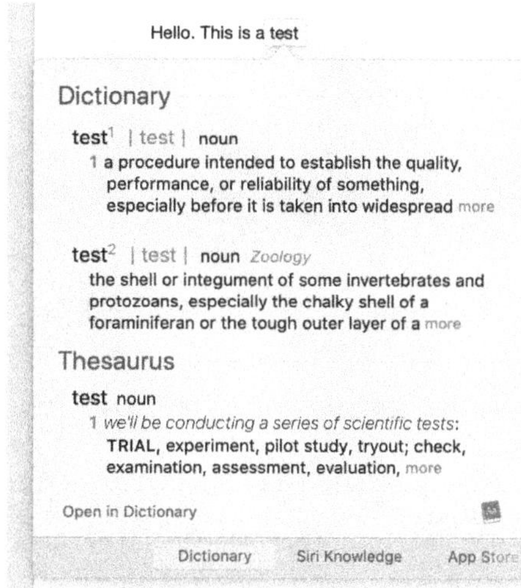

Copy Style

The Style command lets you copy and paste styles, like the Microsoft Word format painter feature. If you ever want to make a piece of text look like another, just select the text with the format you'd like to copy, click Format > Copy Style; then select the text you want to alter and click Format > Paste Style. This can be a major time saver!

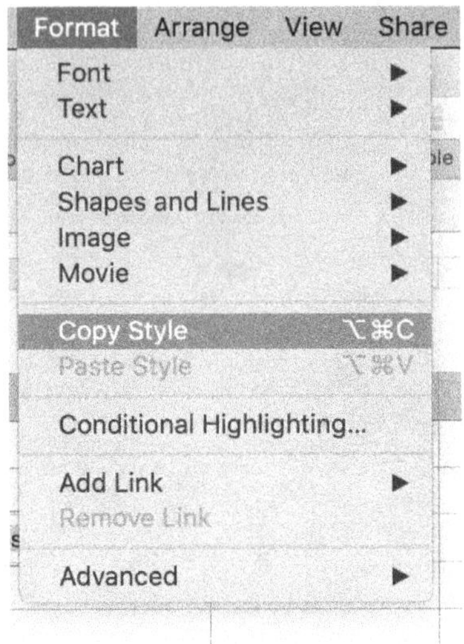

INSERTING HYPERLINKS

If you want to insert a hyperlink to an internet resource, just type out the link. Numbers automatically detects hyperlinks and will insert the link for you. To edit the link or to change the displayed text, just click the link and then tap Link Settings. Here you can edit the link itself, change the text displayed, or remove the link altogether.

If you aren't typing a web address but want to link the text to a web address (for example, you are typing: "I go to UCLA" and you want to provide a hyperlink to UCLA), then select the word you want to hyperlink and click with two fingers to bring up the options. From here, just click Add Link and select the kind of link you want to add. You can edit and remove it the same way as in the previous paragraph.

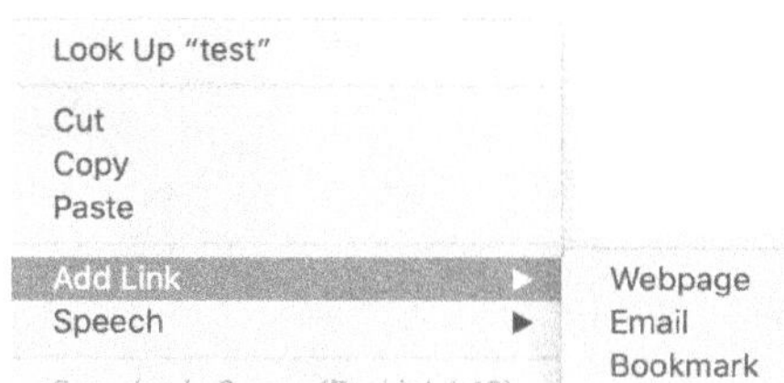

UNDO/REDO

If you mess up (for example you delete a paragraph that you shouldn't have) you can Undo it by going to Edit > Undo; you can also redo it under the same menu.

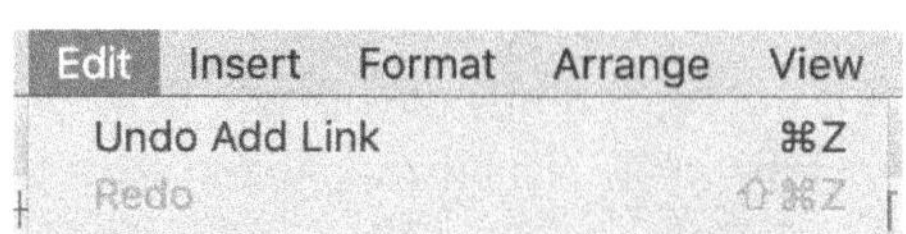

THE FORMATTING TOOLBAR

There are a few menu options to work with in Numbers, but in this section, we will be covering the Formatting Toolbar, which is on the right side of your document.

The Format menu has four tabs across the top: Table, Cell, Text, Arrange.

The first tab, Table, is where you go to change the look of the overall table. For example, if you want to add a border to it. You can also set the size of the rows and columns.

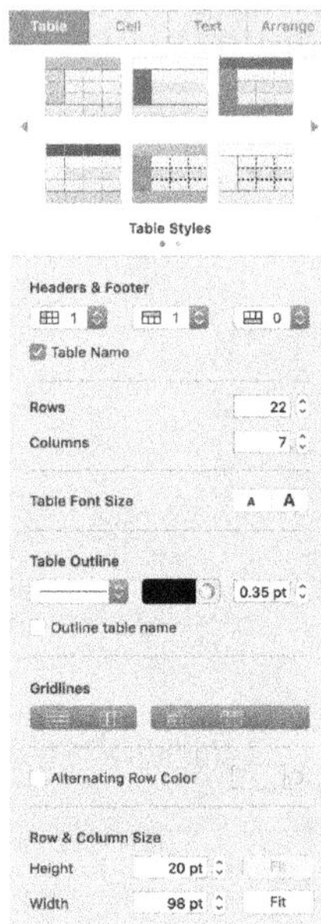

This is also where you can add more rows and columns; this is something distinctively different than Excel. In Excel, you get a spreadsheet that seems like it has endless rows; in Numbers, you get a handful, but can add more. You can do this manually by clicking once on the = button at the bottom of the last row, or to the side of the last column.

The next tab is the Cell options. Where the previous tab made changes globally to the entire table, this menu focuses on cells. You can, for example, select what kind of value the cells have (i.e., they should be formatted like dates or currency); you can also select the type of borders (if any) the cells should have.

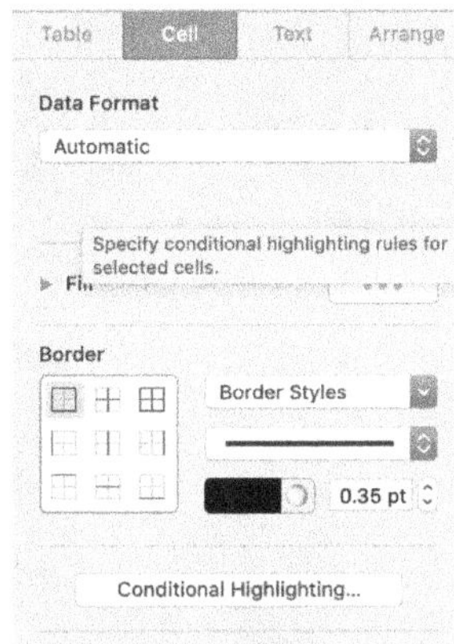

Under the Text tab, it will say "Body" by default. When you click it, you'll see several options. "Body" is normal text in a document—the text you are reading right here would be considered Body Text. Documents have several types of paragraph text; for example, each section of this chapter has a "Heading"—you could just change the font size and make it "look" like a heading, but using a Paragraph Style tells Numbers what kind of text it is so it can put together a table of contents later.

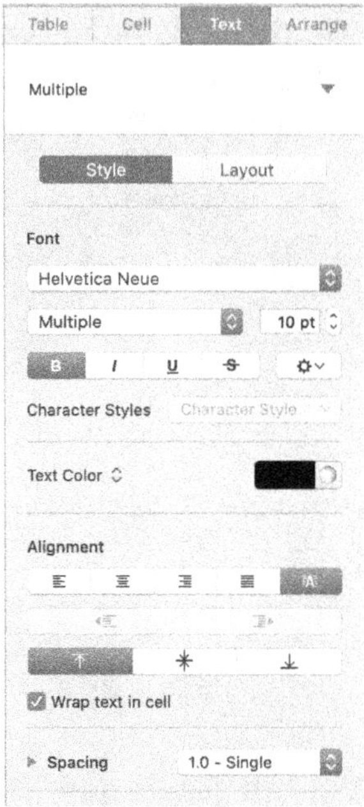

Some of the styles will not be very common, "Label Dark" for example.

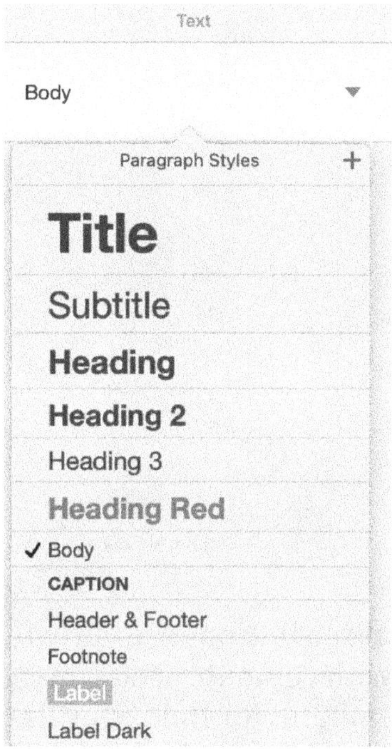

Under this are options for Style, Layout, and More. Let's stay on Style for now, so the next option is Font.

It says 11pt Helvetica; this is the font. If you tap on it, you'll be able to select a new font and adjust the size. Numbers offers a healthy font selection, including perennial favorites like Arial, Times New Roman, and Helvetica. Some notable absences include Comic Sans (and yet Papyrus still made the cut!), Calibri, and Cambria.

The "regular" dropdown shows you all the style choices for that font (some fonts have different options).

The next three buttons are fairly standard. If you're not familiar with computerized word processing, though, remember B for Bold, I for Italic, and U for underline. The S with a line through it puts a strike across any text you type.

Below this are your alignment buttons. Tap them for options to align your text left, center or right, or justify it. Justified text is text that fills one line exactly. Try it out to see how it works.

The next two buttons are indent buttons. Use them to indent, or to move backwards through indents.

Finally, below this is where you can add bulleted lists and line spacing (if you want to double space, for example).

The last tab is the Arrange menu. The Arrange menu makes a little more sense when you see how photos work in the next chapter. The thing you should know here, however, is that you should think of your spreadsheet as an object on a canvas. If you put a photo in front of it, you can go here to make the spreadsheet go in front of or behind the photo—just like you would any other object.

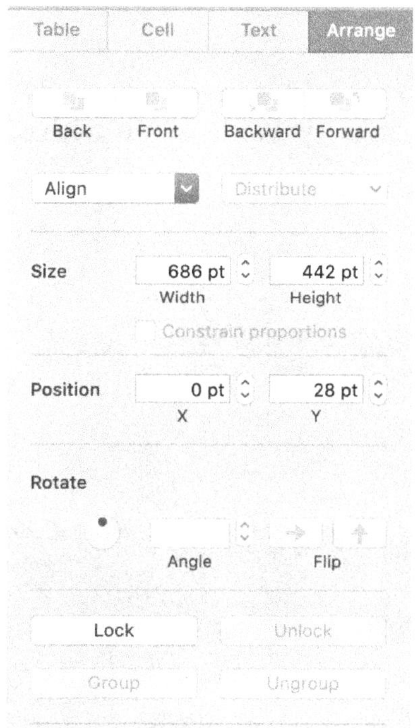

Fun With Functions

Now that we've had some fun, let's get serious and learn about functions.

What is a function, exactly? Functions is basically making calculations. It lets you add up rows, see the average, and so much more.

You tell Numbers that you intend to do a Function when you hit the equals (=) key. This brings up a functions command box.

It also brings up a side menu with a list of over 250 functions!

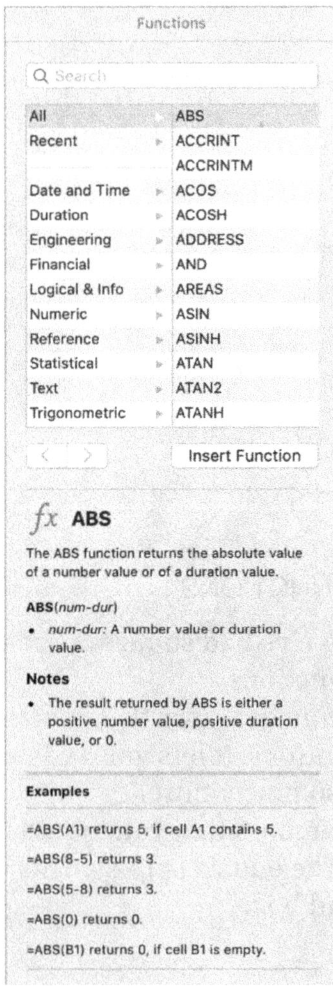

There are obviously a lot of functions! You can also see these functions on Apple's website: https://www.apple.com/mac/numbers/compatibility/functions.html

How Do Functions Work?

Functions can be quite complicated...but they can also be ridiculously easy. While there are functions that will make your head spin trying to figure them out, there are lots of functions that will be second nature to you.

You can use functions like a calculator, for example. Try it. Type "=2*3".

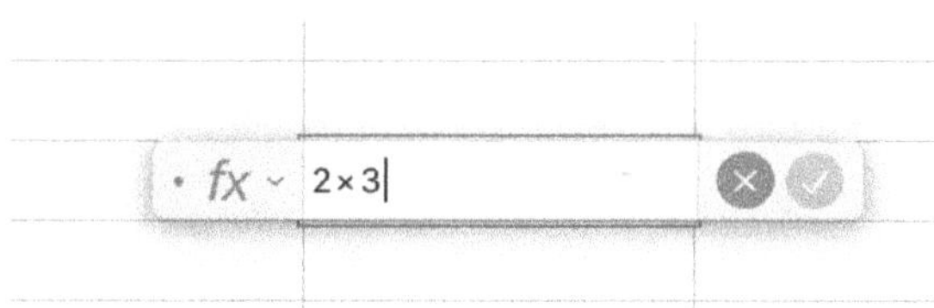

Once you hit enter on your keyboard (or click the green button), you should get 6.

The only equation that might be confusing if you've never used functions is divisions; there is no divide key on the keyboard. So if you want to divide, use the slash key "/".

You can make the equation as easy or as complicated as you want. In the example below, I am using parenthesis for a longer problem.

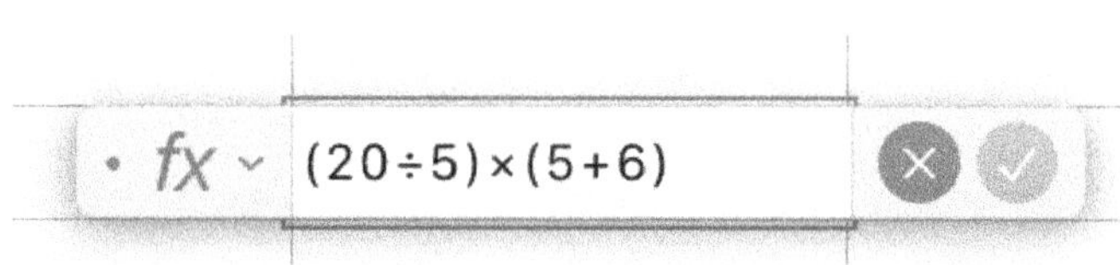

If you do something wrong, you'll get an orange triangle; you can click on the triangle and see what it doesn't like.

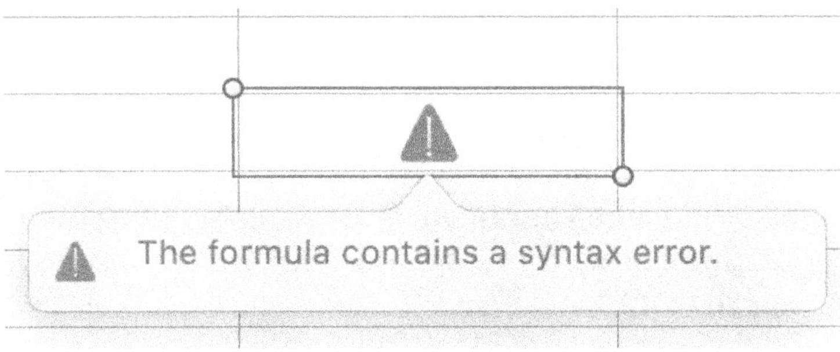

That's all nice, but couldn't you just use a calculator?! Yes! But functions really start to come in handy when you use them with the content that's in your table.

As an example, let's say you have a column of numbers and you want to add them all up.

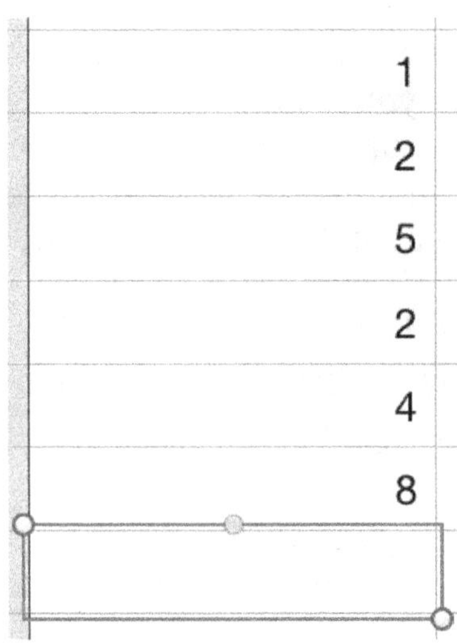

In this example, I'm going to put the sum under them, but there's no rule about this: you can do the formula wherever you want. Just hit the = key, then type "sum" and highlight what you want to add up.

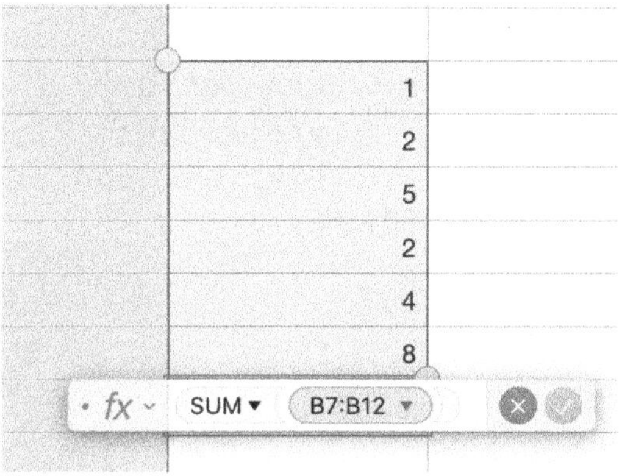

You can also hit the Command button on your keyboard and only select certain cells.

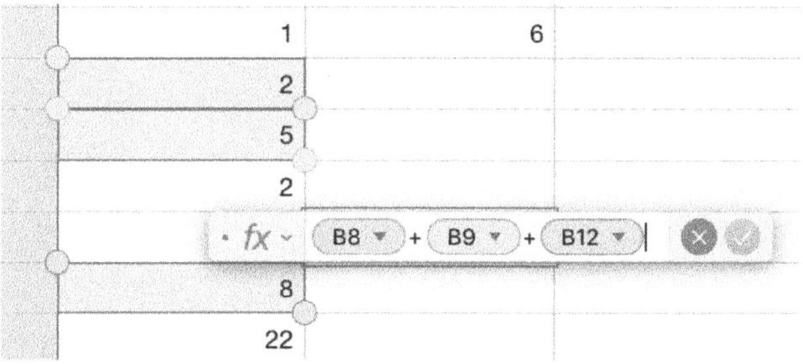

Because this is a beginner's guide, I won't cover advanced functions. Here are the basic ones that you should know:

- Average (shows the average number in a range of numbers)
- Median (shows the median number in a range of numbers)

- Min (finds the smallest number in a selected range)
- Max (finds the largest number in a selected range)
- Count (this is useful if you have numbers and text in a range; count will count all the cells with numbers for you)
- Round (if you are dealing with a lot of decimals, this can help you round to a smaller decimal point)

YOUR TABBED LIFE

Numbers borrows from most other spreadsheet applications, so it should be no surprise that you can have multiple worksheets within a document.

To add a new tab, just click the + button above the default sheet (hint: it's to the left of the tab that says "Sheet 1")

This creates a second tab (by default, it will be called "Sheet 2"). You can now toggle between two worksheets. When you start doing formulas, you can also go into another worksheet and use a figure from there (for example, you could add the cell in worksheet 1 with the cell of worksheet 2).

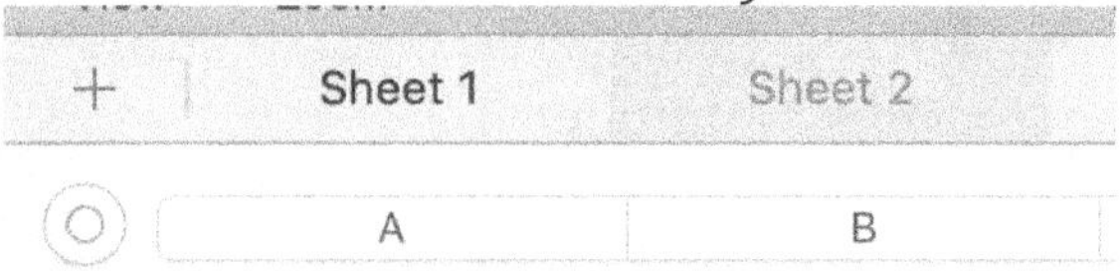

You can rename any of the worksheets by right clicking and clicking rename. In the same area, you can also delete, copy or duplicate the worksheet.

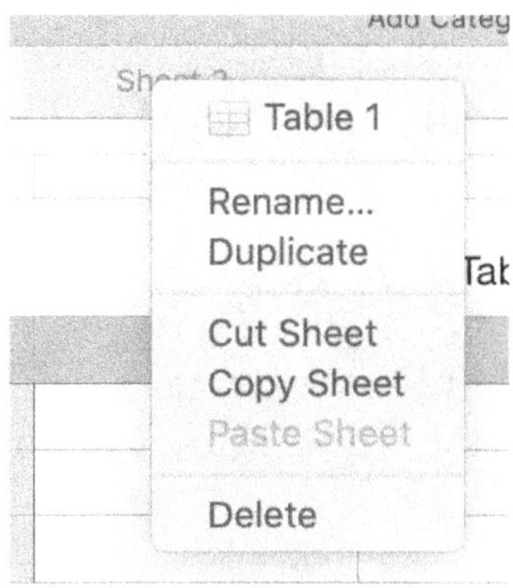

Opening Numbers From iCloud

Numbers can be run right from your browser; it's great for editing, but for intensive design work, the best solution will be your computer.

To access it from your browser, head to iCloud.com and sign in with your Apple ID.

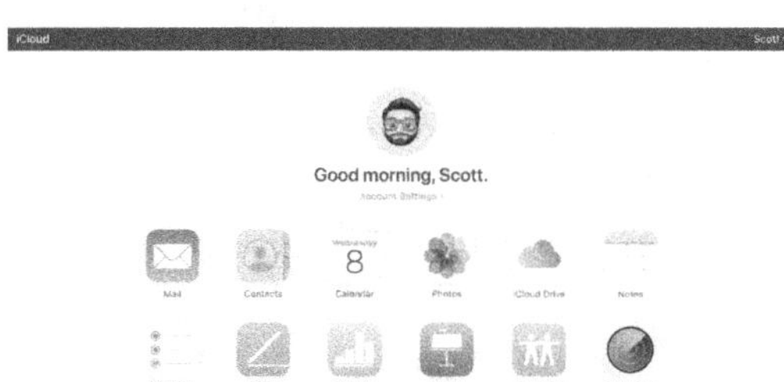

The first screen you'll see will show you all the things you can do from the cloud; one of them is using Numbers. Click it once to open it.

As long as you've been saving your work to the cloud, then any recent docs will show up here and you can click on their thumbnail once to open them.

You can additionally start a new Doc by clicking on the + button in the upper right corner. This will open up Numbers for iCloud. All the features covered in this book can be found in Numbers for iCloud as well.

MANAGING DOCUMENTS

Saving in Numbers is pretty straightforward—especially if you've used Windows before. It's under File > Save.

Before we move forward with using other features in Numbers, I want to go over the less straightforward ways to manage documents.

RENAMING DOCUMENTS

Renaming documents is very easy. Like with many things in Numbers, there's more than one way to do it.

The easiest way is when your document is open; just click on the name in the top center of the document.

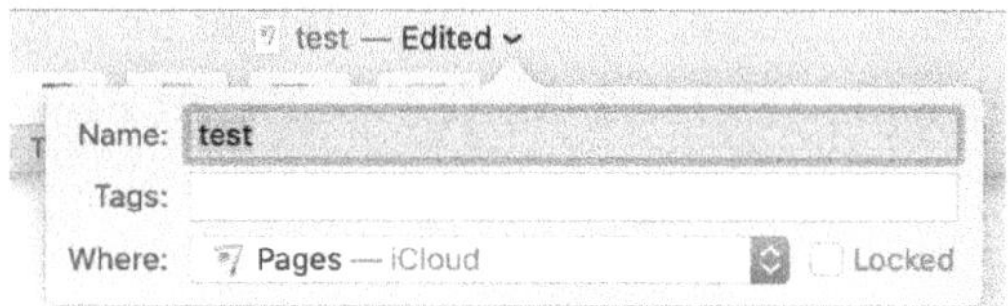

The next way is File > Rename.

The third way is to find it in Finder, click with two fingers, and select Rename.

PRINTING

Printing in Numbers is a little different from other programs. It's in the same place (File > Print), but the print mode looks a bit different.

Since spreadsheets can be quite large, one handy feature in this mode is content scale; this will adjust how large the sheet is so it fits on one or two pages of paper. It will make the content smaller, however.

[2]
PHOTOS FOR NUMBERS

This chapter will cover:

- Insert image
- Arrange / Rotate / Wrap image
- Edit Mask / Alpha
- Image Styling

As much as possible, I'm trying to make learning Numbers fun; there's no better way to make something fun than with photos!

As we go, we'll be learning more about styling tips, but before we get there, we are going to learn about photos—not just about inserting them into the document, but about how to apply more advanced techniques to them.

INSERTING AN IMAGE

Inserting an image can be done several ways. You can copy and paste an image into the spreadsheet, you can drag a photo into the spreadsheet, or you can pick it manually.

To pick it manually, you can go to Insert > Choose, and then find the file location.

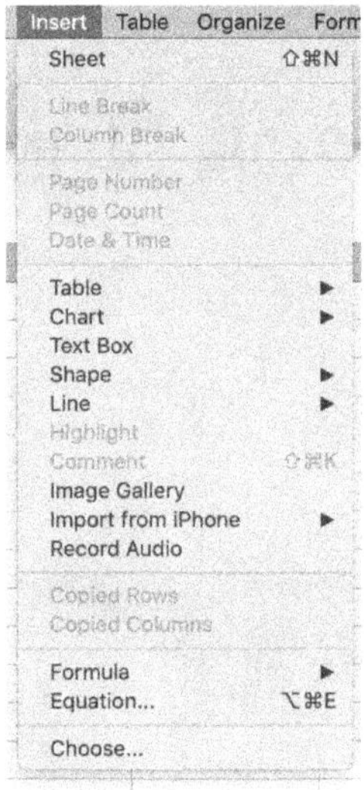

The quicker way to add a photo, however, is from the menu. Click the image button, which shows you all the different media types you can add. You can get photos by clicking on Photos or Image Gallery (if the photos are in your gallery) or by clicking "Choose" to pick where the photo is located.

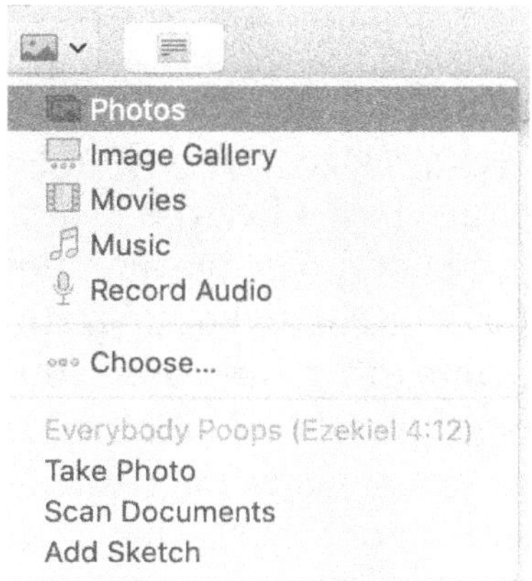

If you pick photos, it's not going to show you all of your photos—just the photos in that photos area of your Mac. You could, for example, have a photo on your USB drive. If that's the case, then you'd want to pick "Choose" from the previous menu instead of photos.

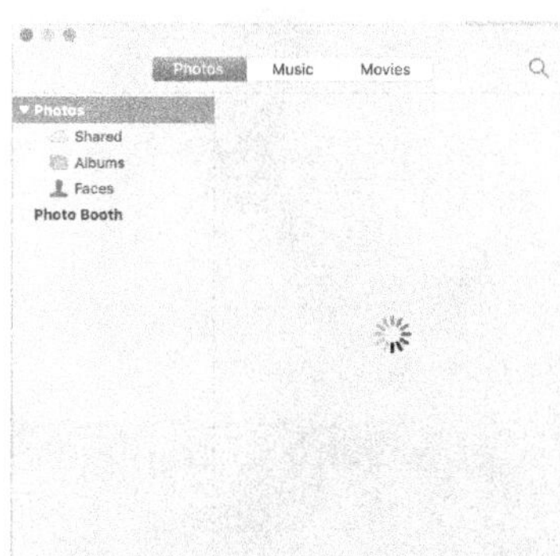

ARRANGING IMAGES

Resize and Rotate

Once your image is inserted, you can use your mouse to move it, resize it, and rotate it. Resizing is pretty straightforward. Click the image, then move to the corner or side of the image and move the little squares on the edges in and out. To rotate the image you'll do the same thing, but when you get to the corner of the image, press the Command key on your keyboard. This will show you a curved line and also show you the percentage of the rotation as you move the image.

Hint: Looking for images? I often use a website named pexels.com to find public domain (or free to use) images.

There's one more way to rotate an image. When you click on the image, you'll notice that the side panel that you used to format text has changed. It's now a new menu with controls to format an image.

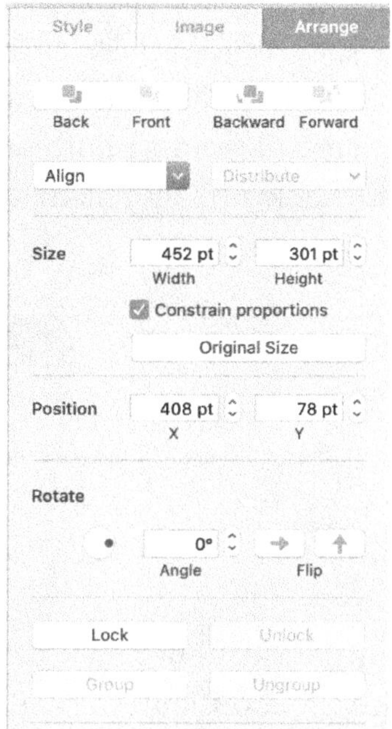

There are three buttons on top of this menu (Style, Image, Arrange); we'll go over the first button in the next section, but for this section, go to Arrange.

On the bottom of this menu, there's a section called Rotate; angle is what you want to use here. The mouse is a quick and easy way to rotate your image, but if you want precision, then this is the best method. Next to the Angle button, you can also vertically and horizontally flip the image using the arrows.

The next set of options let you pick the size of the image; again, you can do this manually with your mouse, but this lets you be a little more precise.

Finally, the last option lets you pick the placement of the image—if you want it in the middle of the page, for example.

WATERMARK

There's no "official" watermark feature, but you can use the Arrange tab to send a photo behind the spreadsheet (using the back / front, backward / forward buttons)

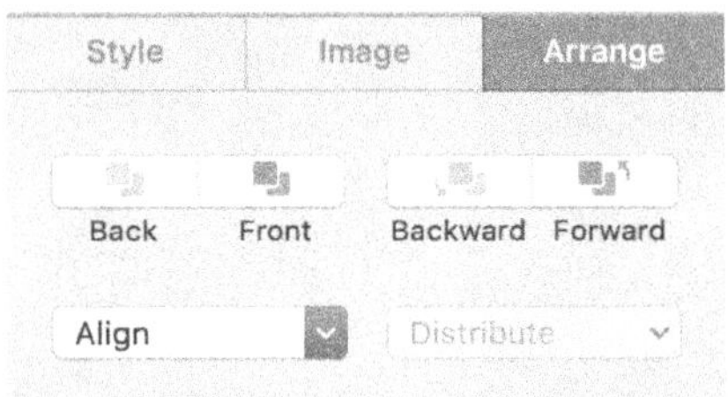

The problem is the photo will probably make the numbers on the sheet difficult to read.

The quick fix is to click the Style menu tab and lower the Opacity.

This makes the image somewhat transparent, which will make text in front of it much easier to see.

IMAGE GROUPING

There's one last section that's greyed out. Grouping. Grouping is greyed out because you need two images to use it.

Add a second image, then click the image, press command on your keyboard, and select the second image; the Group option is no longer greyed out. What grouping does is put two images together, so that when you edit the size, rotation, etc., you are treating the two photos as one image.

If you want to edit just one image, you don't have to ungroup it. You can double click the image to tell Numbers that you want to keep them grouped, but that you want to make changes to one photo while they are grouped.

Edit Mask and Alpha

With your image selected (note: if the images are grouped, you need to double click the image you want to edit—you can't edit both images at the same time), then select the Image button.

This brings up options for image enhancements. At the bottom is the Adjustments section; this section is pretty self-explanatory - the Exposure and Saturation sliders will change the amount of exposure / saturation in the image. The Enhance button will do an auto enhancement based on what the computer thinks the image should look like (the reset button will undo it).

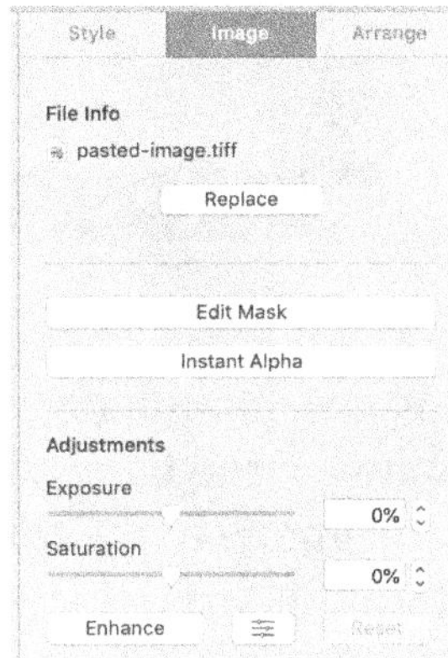

Next to the Enhance button is a control button; this will bring up more adjustment controls.

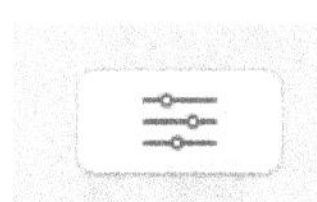

Most people probably won't need this many controls, but it's helpful to know they are there.

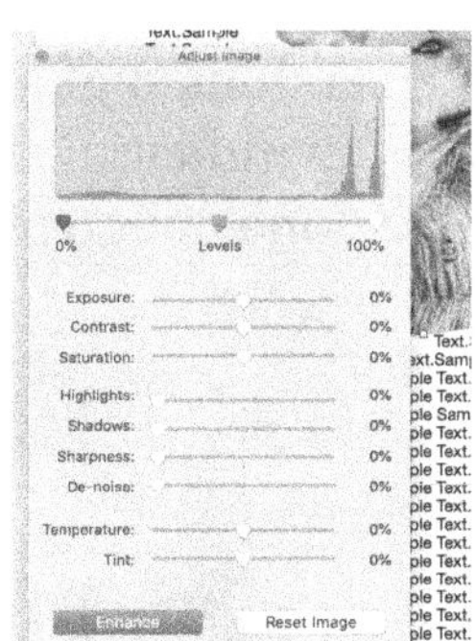

The section that may not be as easy to understand is the top section: Edit Mask and Instant Alpha.

Edit Mask is essentially an image crop. You can use this to cut off parts of the image without resizing it.

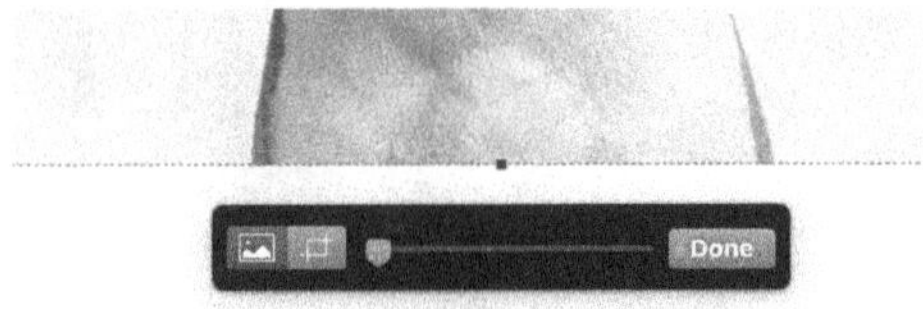

Instant Alpha is one of my personal favorite image editing tools. It removes the background of the image. It's great when your image has a very solid background (you're standing against a solid color wall, for example).

One you click on it, the cursor turns to a square box and you click and drag over the areas you want to take out.

As you click, the sections that are removed will turn a different color to indicate what has been removed. When you're done, let go of the mouse and click the done button.

As you remove the background, it is also autocropping; so if you've removed the background from the top, the image has automatically been cropped to accommodate for it.

STYLING YOUR IMAGE

Now that we know how to move an image around, let's add some style to it.

To style your image, tap the image. Style is the first button on the image edit menu.

Basic Styles

The top box lets you add quick, pre-defined image styles to your image. For example, if you want your image to have a box around it.

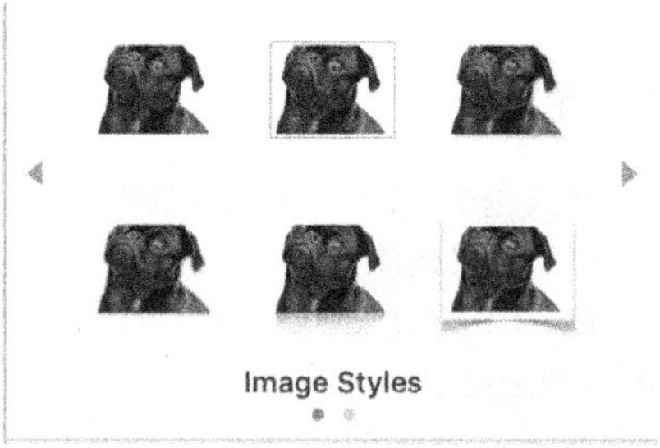

Most people will probably want to do manual editing to the photo, but if you use the arrow in this section, you'll notice a + button. Once you manually make changes to the image (add your transparency, borders, etc.), you can use this button to save these changes, so you can apply them to another photo that you want to have a similar look and feel.

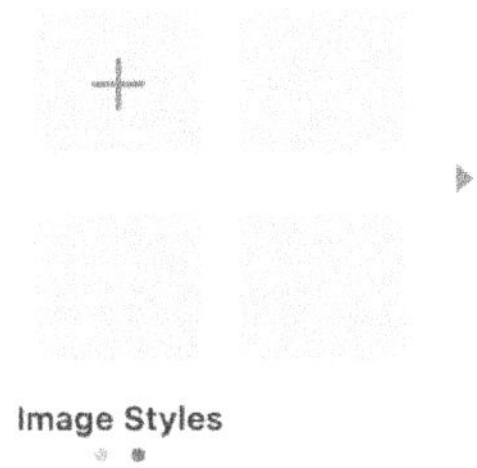

Border

The next section is the Border; there is no border on the image by default. If you click the box with the red diagonal line, it will show a dropdown of all the different styles available.

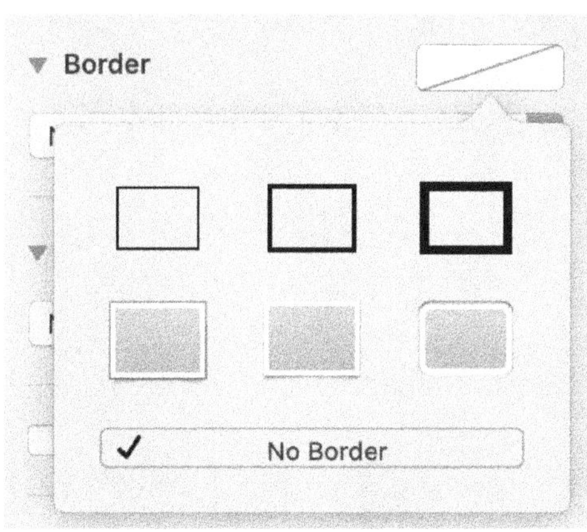

Once you pick your border style, you'll be able to adjust the weight of the border using the slider.

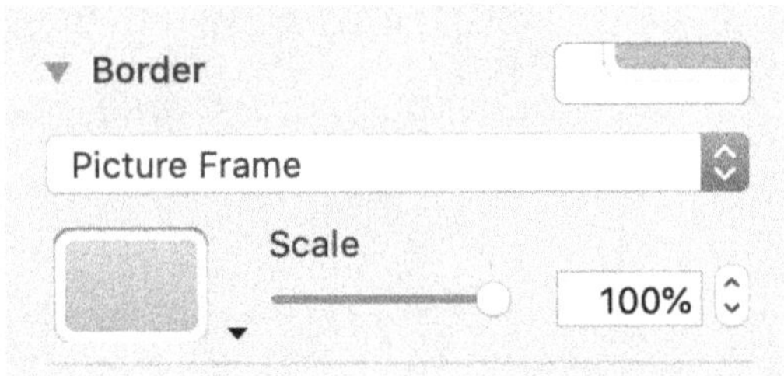

If you click the preview of the border, you will also see all the different border styles available for the style that you have picked. Styles vary depending on the style you are using.

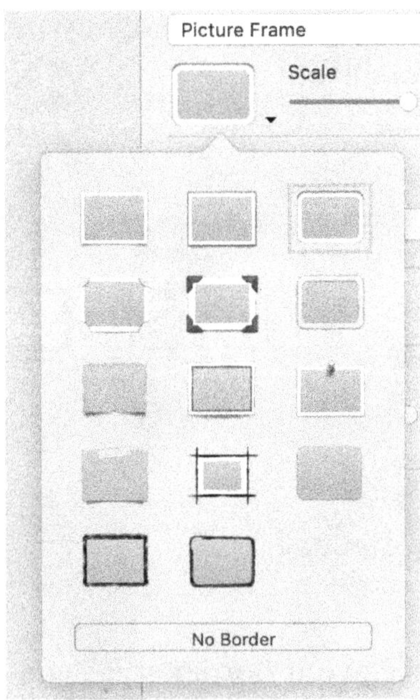

SHADOW

Shadows can add a little more dimension to your photo and help it pop off the page more. It works very similarly to Borders; click the thumbnail with the red line through it, then pick the shadow style.

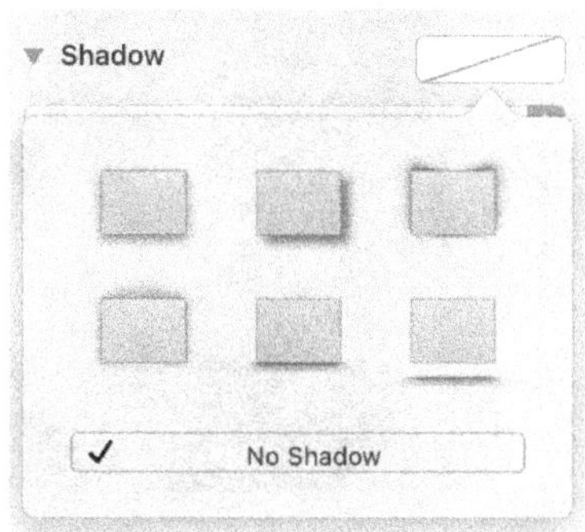

Once you pick the style, you'll get several shadow options to increase or decrease the amount of shadowing used.

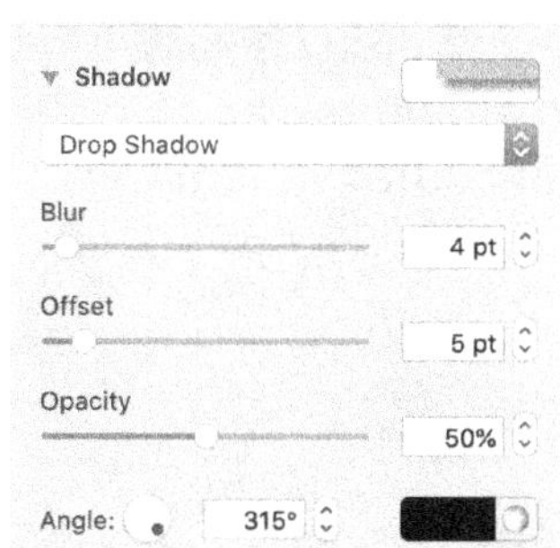

As you make changes, the image will change in real-time, so you immediately see the effects. Notice in the image below how the image has a more 3D look?

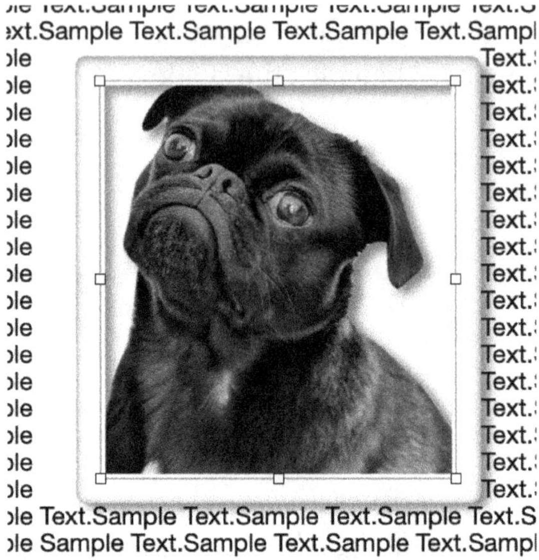

Reflection

Reflection is a simple check / uncheck box; you can use the slider to adjust the amount of reflection used, but that's the only edit available.

You can see in the example below how the reflection gave the image the appearance of an image reflecting on the page (the reflection is the darker area on the bottom of the image).

Transparency

The final style change is transparency. Transparency makes an image more see-through (see the example below). This is great for something like a watermark, but doesn't help a lot if you don't have something below the image.

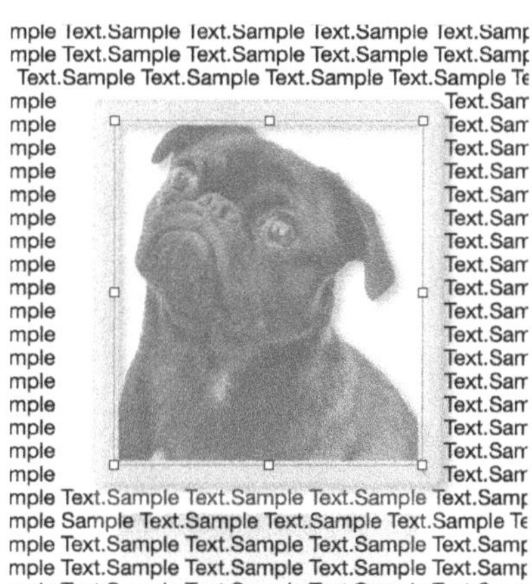

In the below example, I put the transparent image above another photo to illustrate how you can use it on top of another image.

[3]

MANAGING TABLES

This chapter will cover:

- Inserting a table
- Styling a table
- Deleting a table

Numbers is a little different from Excel. You aren't looking at a spreadsheet in Numbers. You're looking at a "table".

What's the difference? At first glance, not a lot. But once you start playing around with tables, you'll notice there are differences. The biggest is that you can have multiple tables in your document. If you wanted to do that in Excel, you'd just open another tab (which you can also do in Numbers).

The below image illustrates two tables in the same workbook (or document). Because they're objects, they can easily be moved around.

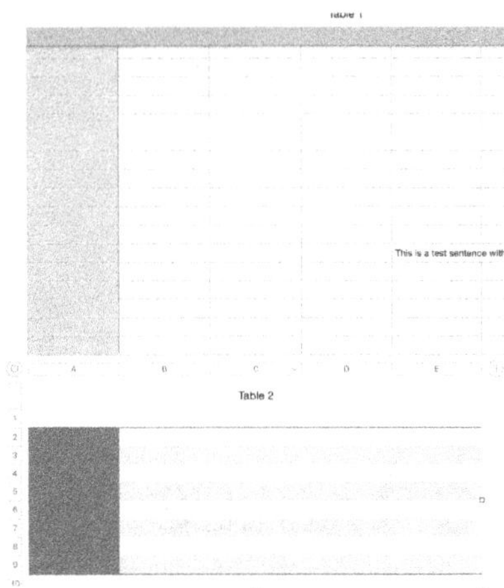

Inserting a Table

If you have ever added a table in Word, then you may be used to picking the size and width before adding the table; in Numbers, you add the table and then adjust it accordingly.

To add a table, tap the Table button from the top menu bar (you can also use Insert > Table from the menu options at the top of MacOS). You'll have several styles to pick from, but again, this is different from Word where you drag it to the number of rows and columns that you want.

Adding Columns and Rows

Your table is now inserted, but chances are it's not the right size.

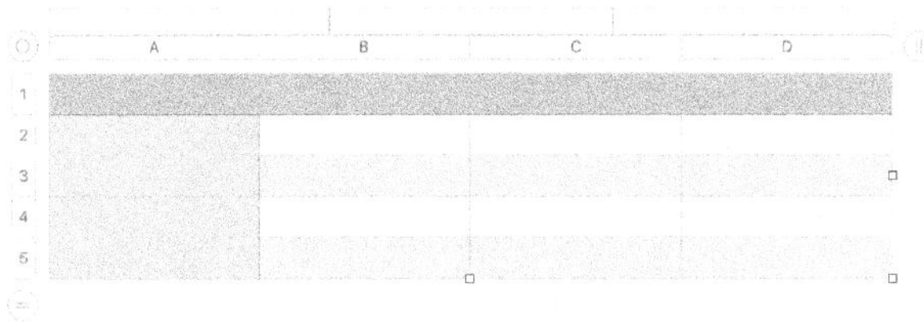

At the bottom of the last row (or the side of the last column) there's a circle with two lines. Click on either of those to adjust the number of columns / rows. You can either use the up / down arrows to pick, or you can click the number and then type the amount you want.

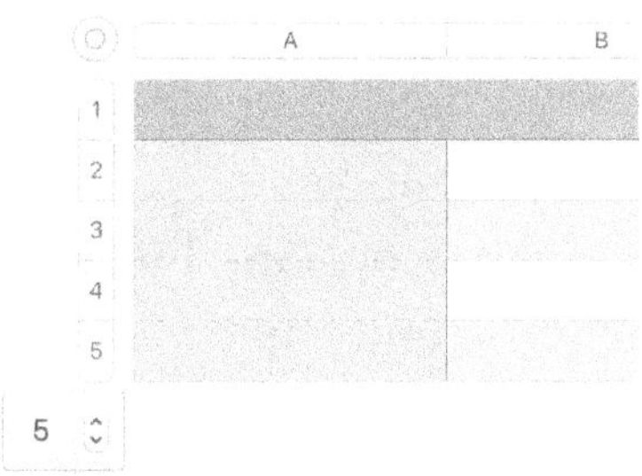

Row / Column Options

If you want to delete or add a row / column, then go to the row or column you want to make changes to, and then click the drop-down arrow. Several options will come up.

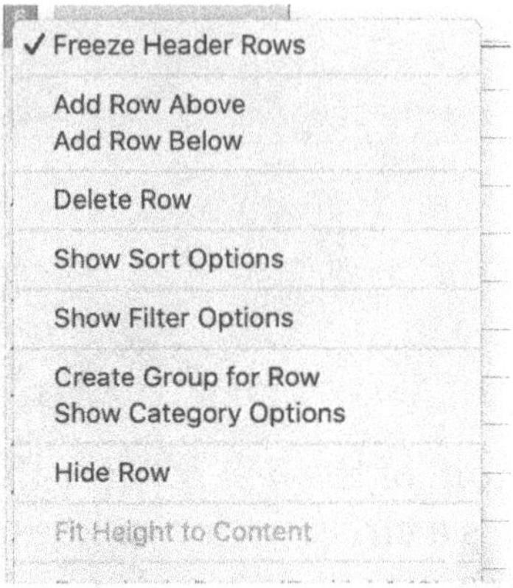

You can also click the number associated with the row / column to select all. This is helpful if you want to copy / paste a row or column.

Table Options

You can see more options by clicking on the Table options in the top menu bar.

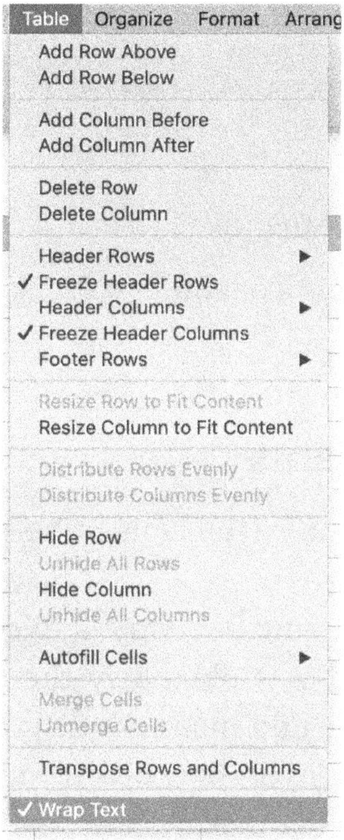

By default, Wrap Text is selected. If you are unfamiliar with text wrap, it means text automatically wraps around the cell like in the example below.

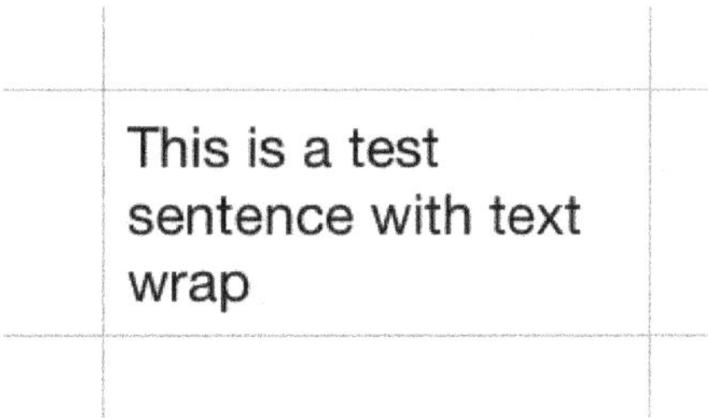

If you turn it off, then it would look like the below example.

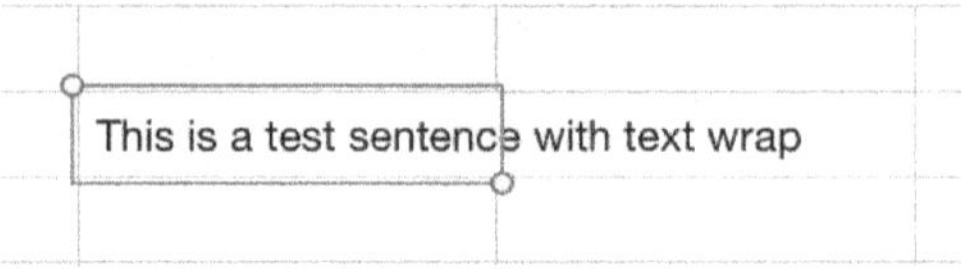

Deleting Tables

Deleting an entire table is a quick process. Click the table. Hit delete.

Importing Tables

Importing a table from somewhere else can be done a few different ways.

The first, and quickest, way is to copy and paste the table. Command V is obviously the easiest way to do this, but go to the Edit menu. Notice there are Paste and Paste and Match Styles options? If you aren't getting the paste results that you want, try this Paste instead.

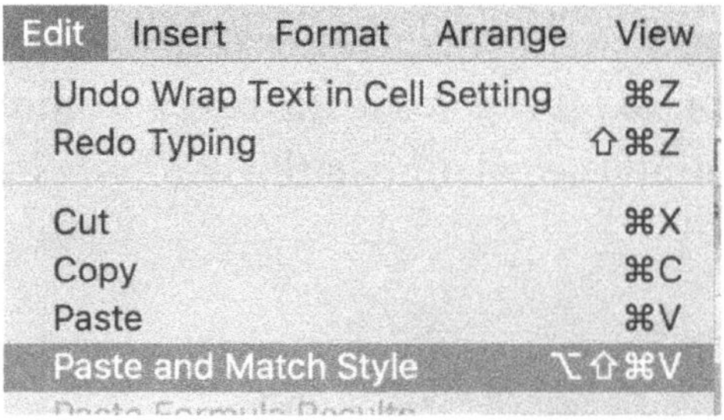

If you don't need to make changes to the table, what a lot of people prefer to do is just make a screenshot of the spreadsheet: Command + Shift + 3 (or Command + Shift + 4 if you want to only select areas of the screen).

[4]
CHARTS

This chapter will cover:

- Inserting a Chart
- Editing Chart Data
- Styling a Chart

Charts can add color and interest to your documents, as well as help you present data more clearly. Numbers includes a powerful Charts feature that allows you to quickly create beautiful, customizable charts that really pop out of the page.

Now that you know how to use Tables, using Charts will be a breeze.

INSERTING A CHART

To insert a chart in Numbers, tap the Insert button, then tap Charts. From here, you'll choose the type of chart (bar, area, line, pie), as well as the style you want. Choose from several different color schemes in 2D, 3D, and interactive. If you change your mind about your chart choice you can always change it later, without losing any data you've entered. Just tap on your favorite chart to insert it into your document.

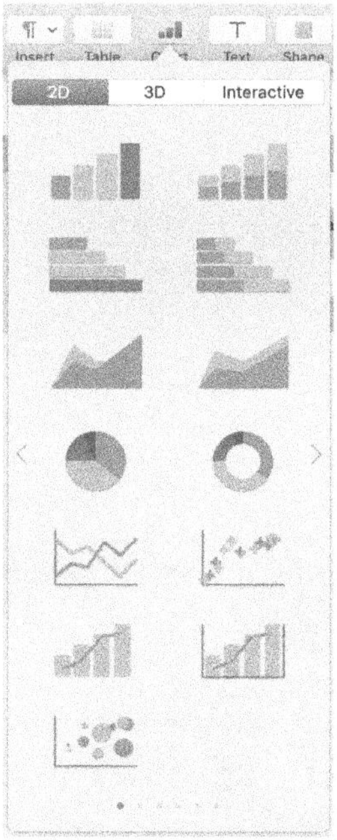

As with almost everything in Numbers, you can also add Charts from the top menu (Insert > Chart).

If you want to show a chart of something that's in your table / spreadsheet, then just highlight it before you insert the chart.

Once you have your chart picked, a chart that's already filled out will be added to your document (I'm using a Pie chart in this chapter, but the same features apply to almost all of the charts—they just look a little different).

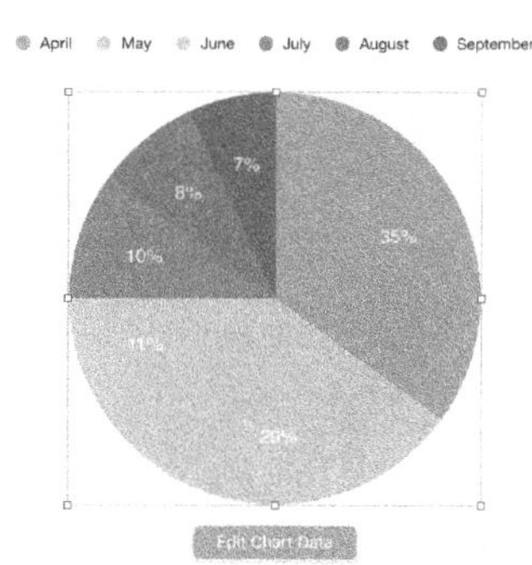

Editing Chart Data

It's so nice for Numbers to put a pretty chart that's all filled out into our document, right? Sure! But wouldn't it be nicer if it had meaningful data? To add your own data, click Edit Chart Data. This brings up a mini table that you can edit with whatever information you want.

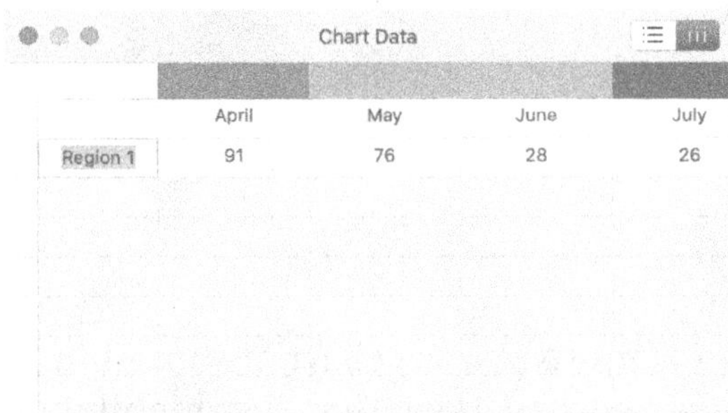

I'm going to replace the months with the names of states, and use an entirely different data range. The chart changes with each change I make in the table. Notice that the chart below is completely different from the one above?

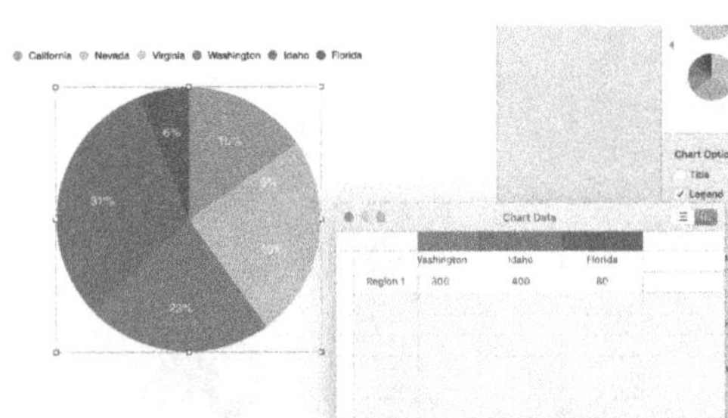

You can enter additional rows if you need to—but this won't work on all charts (like the pie chart).

Styling Your Pie Chart

Now that you have the data you want, it's time to style it.

If you did a pie chart, then you'll see three options on the side (Chart, Wedges, Arrange).

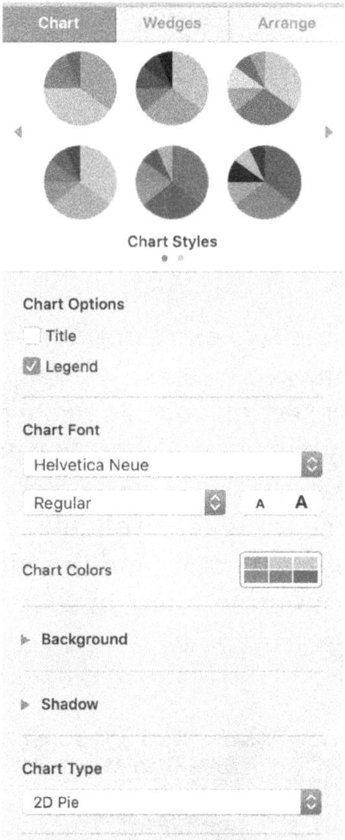

Other charts (like bar charts) have four (Chart, Axis, Series, Arrange).

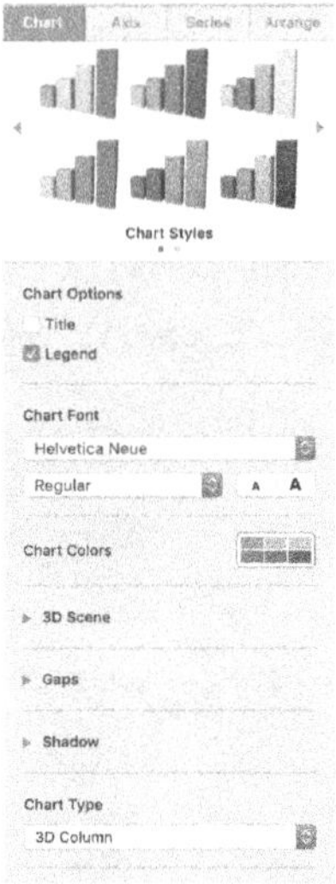

I'll go over the two extra options for a bar chart in the next section.

In the Chart section you can make changes to the entire chart. By default the chart has no title, but if you check off the box, a title (cleverly named "Title") is added to your chart; you'll probably want to name it something else. To do that (and this also applies to re-naming pretty much anything in your chart) double click on it and start typing.

Below the title is where you can change the font, and under that, the chart colors. When you click on the chart colors, it gives you a whole host of pre-defined colors. But what if you want to pick your own?

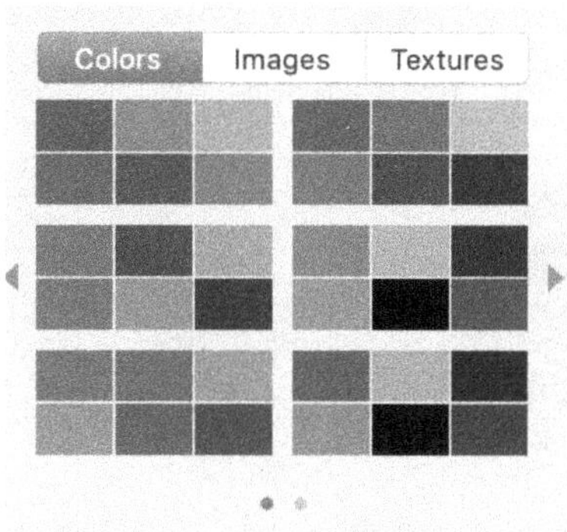

There's one extra small step to picking your own colors. You have to double click on the wedge that you want to change the color of, and then over on the menu options to the right of it, click Style (Style is a new option that's only there if you double click the wedge). From here, you can pick a color under "Fill."

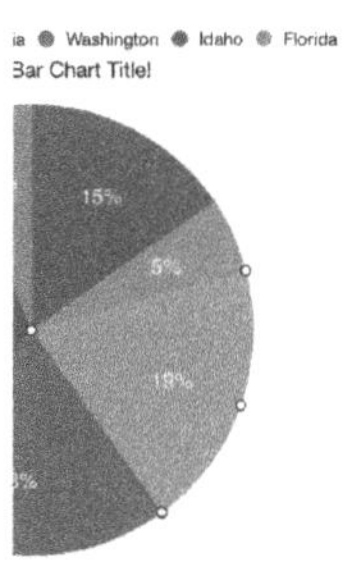

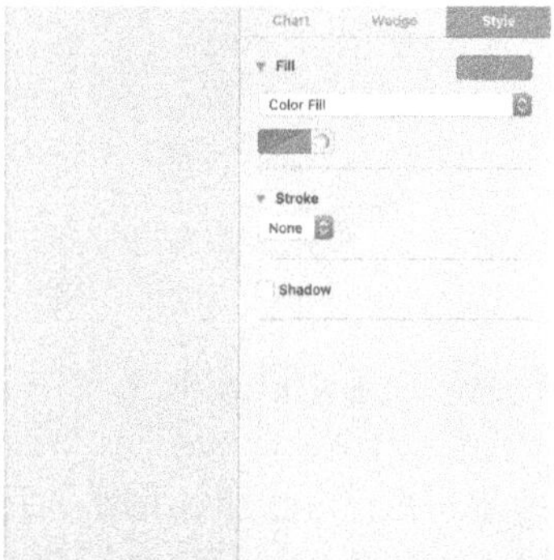

While we are in this section, let's go just under it to Stroke and Shadow. Both of these options help a wedge stand out a little. This is useful if you want to illustrate one area of the chart over others. See in the example below how I added a dotted line (and increased the line weight to 4) and also added a shadow.

If you really want that wedge to stand out, try pulling it apart from the chart. You can do that by clicking on the Wedge option, and then changing the Wedge Position. Look at the example below; the wedge is now separated in the chart.

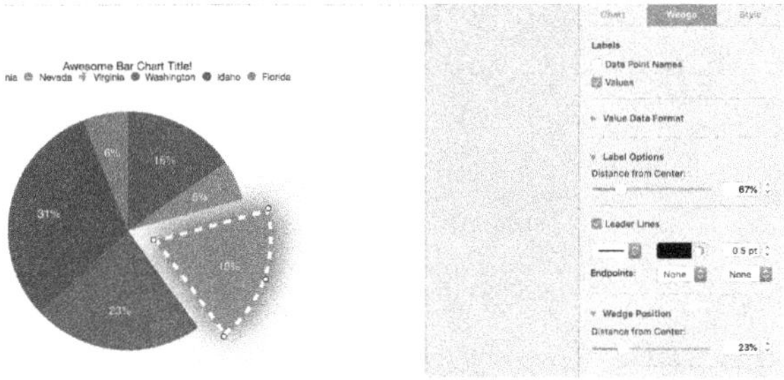

Now let's go back to the chart section and look at the other options we can apply to the entire chart. You can give it a background, add a shadow to it, and finally, change the Chart Type. You can make it a different pie chart or turn it into a line chart (note: this will probably interfere with your data and you may have to redo some of it).

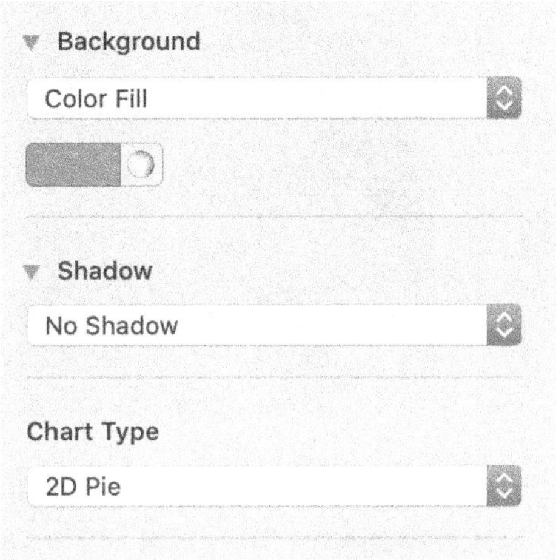

We saw how going to the Wedge section could separate your single wedge from the rest. If you don't double click the wedge and change it, below is what happens.

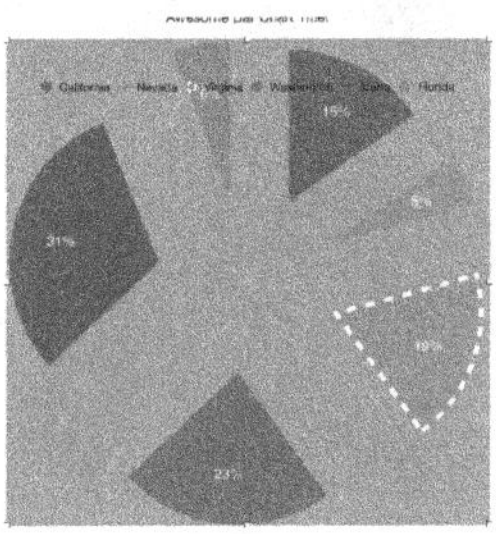

All the wedges separate. If that's what you want, then perfect! If that's not what you want, undo and then double click the wedge you want to separate.

Checking off Data Point Names will put the names of the values in the chart (you can also keep it in the Legend).

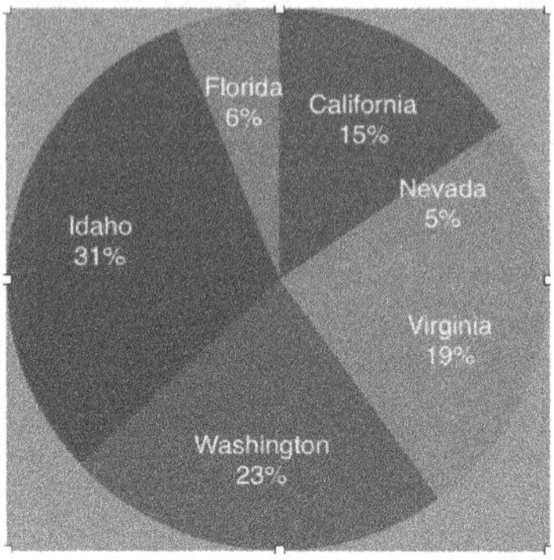

The values on the chart are currently shown as percentages; if you prefer showing them as numbers (or another value type), you can change this under Value Format.

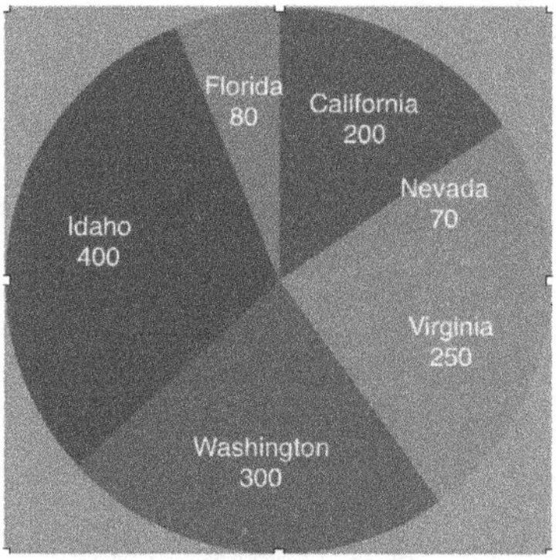

If you check off Lender Lines, you probably won't notice a difference; to see what the lines are, click the Straight drop-down and change it to Angled.

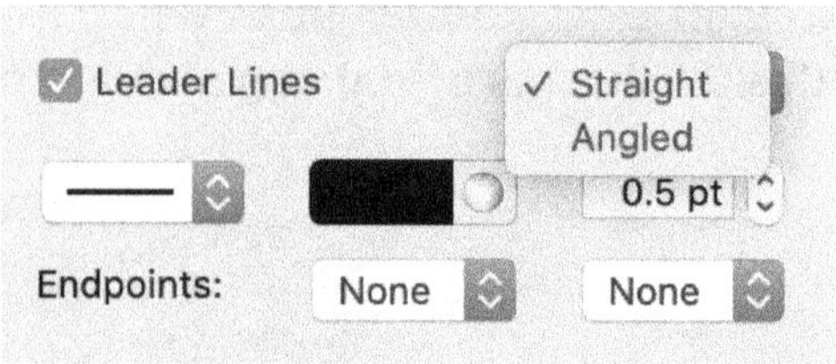

You should now see lines to the sides of the chart.

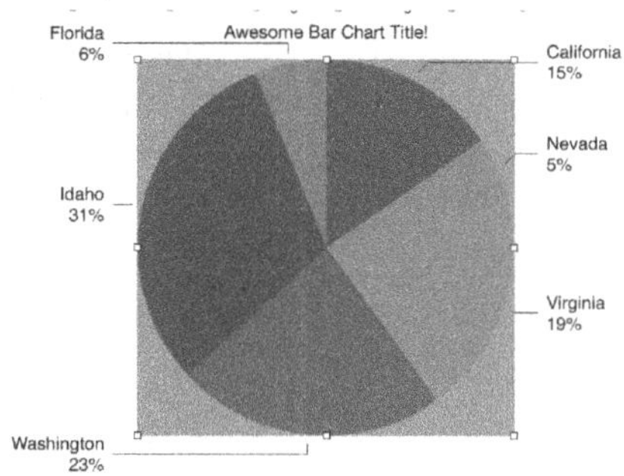

The arrange option should look familiar to you. You've seen it in the Tables section and the Photos section; it's the same features.

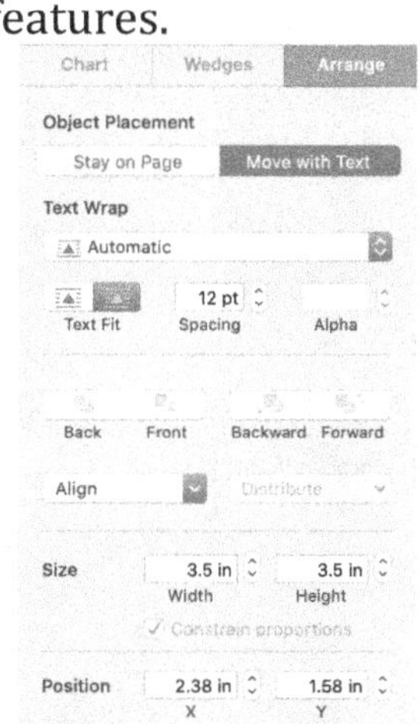

STYLING YOUR BAR CHART

Now that you know how to style a Pie Chart, you'll have no problem with the Bar Chart; it's basically the same, but with more options for labels.

In the axis sub-tab, you can turn category labels, series names, gridlines, and titles on and off. Similarly, in the Y-axis or X-axis sub-tab, you can turn value labels, gridlines, and titles on and off. Here you can also specify the number format you'd like to use and adjust the value scale settings. Number formatting includes the option to add prefixes and suffixes, like currency symbols, or suffixes, like %, millions, etc.

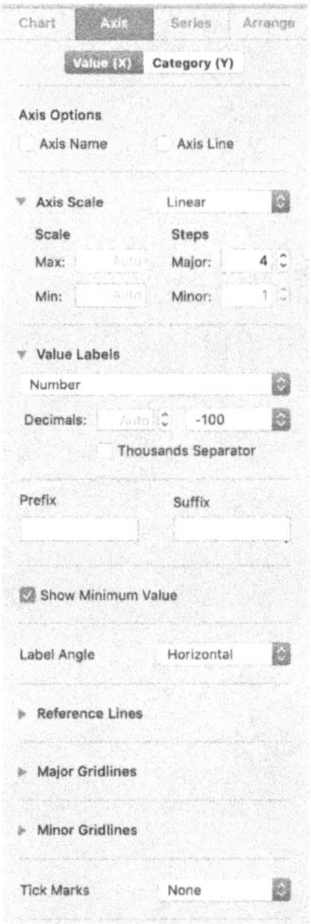

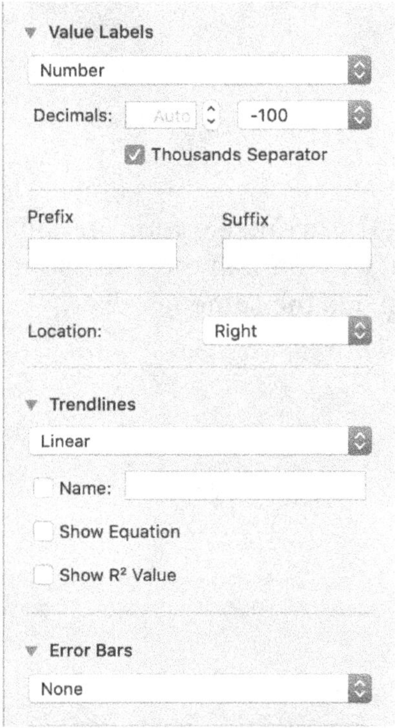

Note: the contents of the sub-tabs change depending on the orientation of your chart. The number formatting option may appear under either the x- or y-axis, depending on the type of chart you've inserted.

[5]

SHAPES

This chapter will cover:

- Inserting a Shape
- Resizing Shapes
- Creating Text Boxes

Pictures are great! They really help your document look snazzy. But there's one more type of graphical illustration you should consider: shapes. Shapes can be great additions to a document – they can be used to draw attention to an area of a document or to illustrate your points graphically. Numbers offers a number of handy pre-made shapes for you to use, and I'll show you how to get the most out of them.

INSERTING A SHAPE

To insert a shape into a document, click the shape button or go to Insert > Shape from the top menu. This will bring up all the shapes available for you. Find the one you like and click it to insert it.

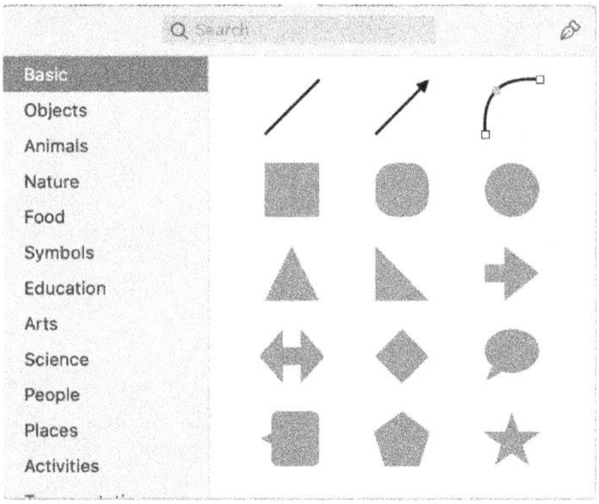

Remember that you can change the color, border and shadow/reflection effects later!

Shapes sounds a little misleading. If you're like me, you're probably thinking square, circle, etc. But shapes in Numbers are kind of like clipart. Yes, basic shapes are there, but so are other things. In the example below I searched for "Dog" and got five results!

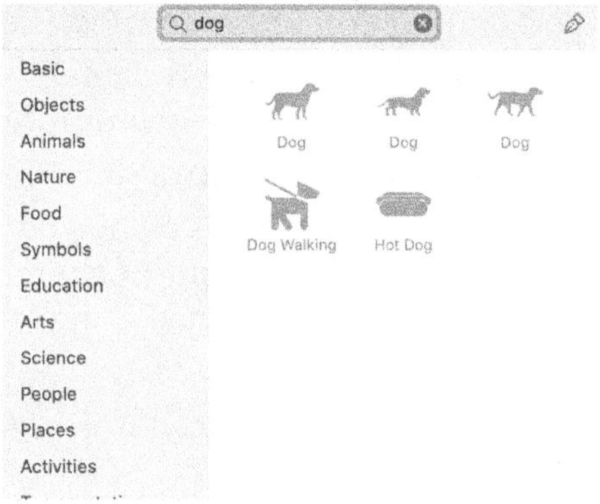

Resizing Shapes and Adjusting Proportions

Shape resizing is just like resizing photos: tap on a corner and drag it to the desired size. However, with Shapes, you can also adjust proportions. What does that mean? It's better shown than explained. Double tap your trackpad on the shape to bring up the shape options. Now click "Make Editable."

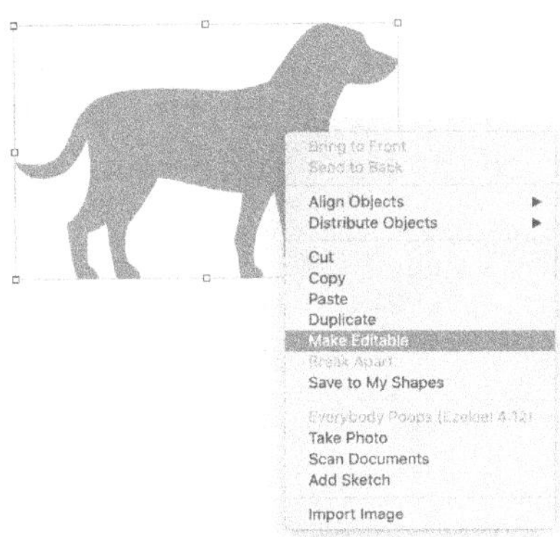

There are now a bunch of dots on the shape. These represent points that you can adjust.

As an example, I moved the point inward from the dog's stomach and look what happened.

By default you make these changes with a curved point, but you can change this by bringing the options up again. Notice the three different points?

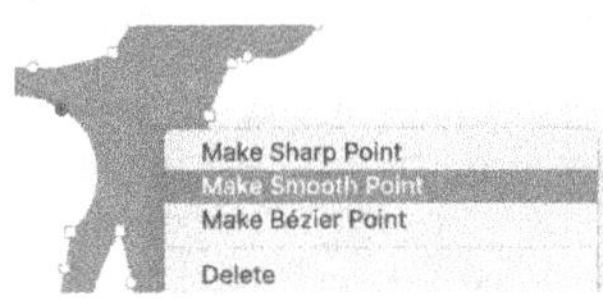

Moving and Rotating Shapes

To move a shape, simply tap on it and drag it to a new location. To rotate a shape, click the image then press the command button—just like you would an image.

Adding Text to a Shape

To add text on top of a shape, double-tap on it to activate its text field. Then just type your text!

CREATING TEXT BOXES

There's one more type of shape, but it's not under shape. It's a Text Box. Text Boxes are exactly what they sound like—floating boxes that have text.

Why use a Text Box instead of typing out the text? Ideally, you want to use them when you are making something like a title—not when you are typing out your epic novel. It's for short text that you want to stand out.

Unlike standard text, Text Boxes are treated in the same way images are, so you can easily move them around and have other things wrap around them.

To get started, click the T in the menu.

You can also do Insert > Text Box.

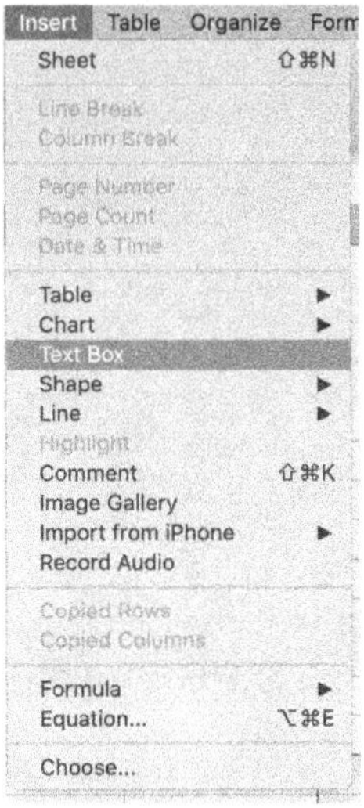

This puts a floating box with generic text in your document.

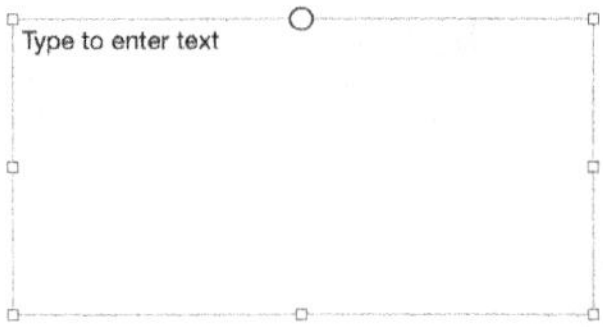

You can change the color of the box and more by clicking on Style; it has all the same types of options that you'd find in the Image or Shape options.

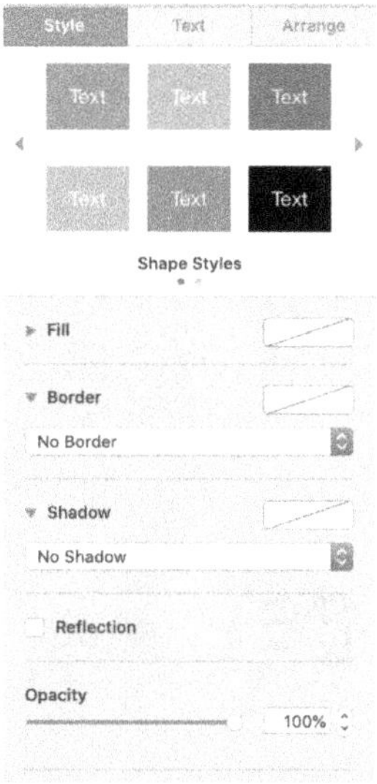

Because it's a Shape, you are able to edit it like you would a shape. In the below example, I curved out the bottom portion of the box.

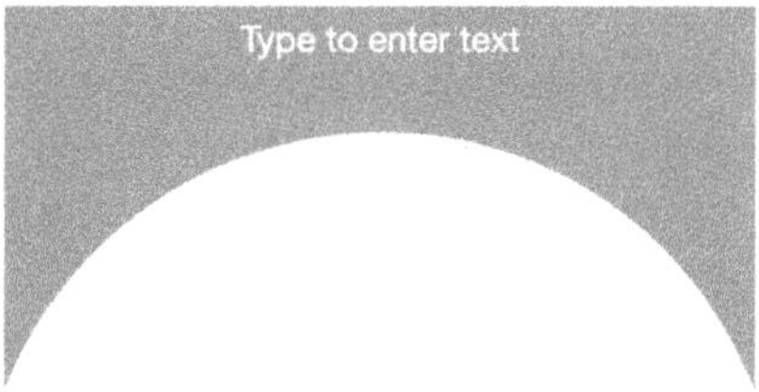

STYLING SHAPES AND TEXT BOXES

Styling Shapes and Text boxes is the same as styling an image, so I won't repeat myself here. If you are confused about styling, refer to the section in the Photos chapter.

[7]
TEMPLATES

This chapter will cover:

- Using third-party Numbers Templates
- Creating your own Templates

Numbers comes with over two dozen templates in five categories - some for calendars, some for reports and professional use, and others for travel planners.

What exactly is a Template? A Template is a document that's already formatted—complete with text and images. Why would you want that? The idea is you delete the text (and replace the images) to make it your own, but save time on the sometimes complicated formatting aspect of it.

Some templates contain multiple tabs.

Now that you understand most of the formatting options available in Numbers, you can use any of these templates as a starting off point. You can change the images, colors, and layout of each template to suit the needs of your project.

USING THIRD-PARTY NUMBERS TEMPLATES

Two dozen templates is a lot, but if you use Numbers long enough, you probably will want a few more; if you get to that place then there are websites (and even apps) which sell Numbers templates (sometimes they are free). A basic web search for "Numbers templates" or even "free Numbers templates" will show you what I mean.

Word of caution: like anything you download, use at your own risk. If a website looks sketchy, be wary of downloading a template.

To use a template like this, just go to the website, find a template you like, and follow the site's instructions to download it to your computer's hard drive.

After that, Numbers can open the template and you can begin to edit it. It is strongly recommended to make a duplicate of your template document before you begin working on it, so that you will continue to have a blank one for later if you need it.

These third-party templates are great for more variety—for example, if you are looking to give your resume a little more creativity.

CREATING YOUR OWN "TEMPLATES"

Unfortunately, Numbers currently does not allow you to save templates in the Create New Document screen. However, you can work around this sorely missed feature by setting up your "template" as a regular Numbers document.

Personally, I make a duplicate of the document (i.e. File > Duplicate) and name it something like "Resume Template."

[8] Sharing and Exporting Documents

This chapter will cover:

- Sharing documents
- Exporting documents

In spite of the popularity of iPhones and iPads, Apple users still often find themselves marooned in a Windows-based world. Numbers is a wonderful program, but it's incomprehensible to Microsoft Excel. Fortunately, Numbers offers several methods for sharing and exporting Numbers documents in multiple formats. Numbers also makes moving documents across Apple devices absolutely effortless, thanks to iCloud.

SYNCING DOCUMENTS WITH ICLOUD

If you've enabled iCloud in your Numbers app, your documents will be synced across your devices automatically, with absolutely no work required on your part. You can even access your documents online from any internet connection at www.icloud.com.

EMAILING A DOCUMENT FROM NUMBERS

E-mailing documents is one of the most straightforward methods of sharing your document. Go to Share > Send a Copy.

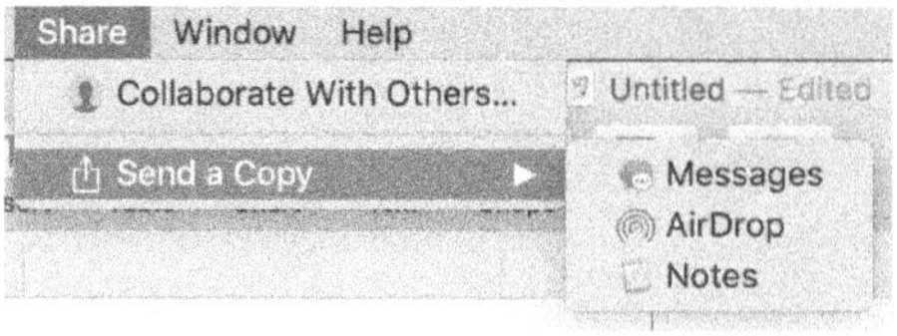

COLLABORATING

You can also collaborate on a document by going to Share > Collaborate With Others.

This brings up an option that asks how you would like to share the document.

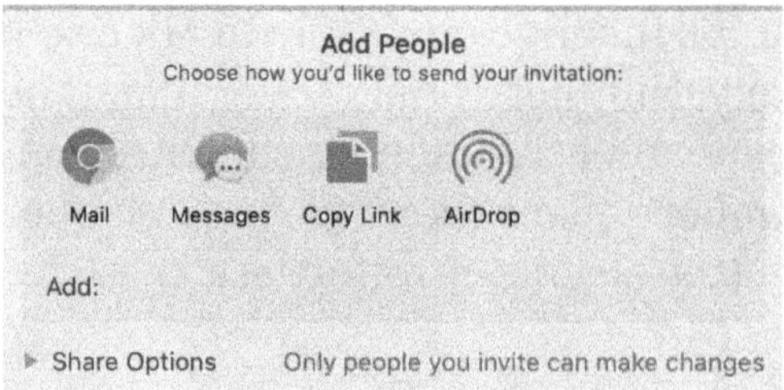

I recommend clicking on the Share Options dropdown to make sure the right permissions are enabled. For example, you can make the document readable to anyone you share it with or anyone who gets the document; you can also give the user permission to make changes.

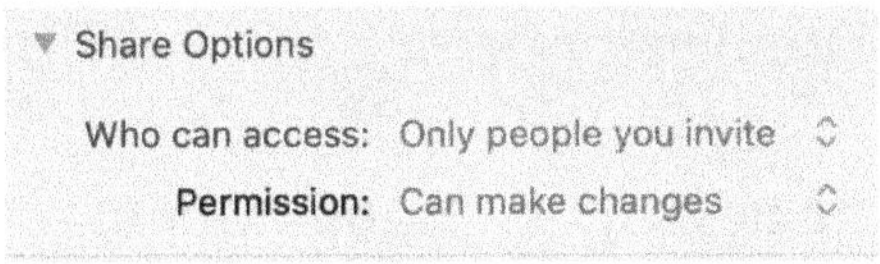

EXPORT A NUMBERS DOCUMENT

By default, you'll be saving your file as a Numbers document. That's great if you have Numbers, but if you're sharing it with (or opening it on) a computer that doesn't have pages, or you want to create a universal PDF that anyone can see, then you'll need to export it.

This is pretty straightforward. Go to File > Export.

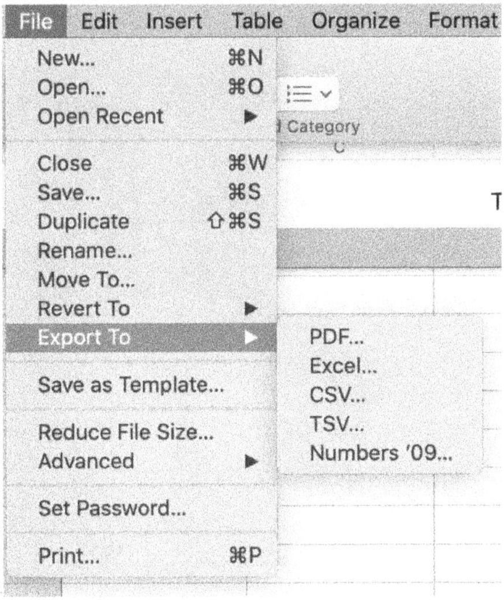

There are five different file types:

- PDF
- Excel
- CSV
- TSV
- Numbers '09

PDF is the best option if you want to preserve all the formatting in the document and make it look exactly as it appears in Numbers.

APPENDIX A: AN EXERCISE IN NUMBERS

By now, you should be familiar with all the basic features of Numbers; before leaving you, I'm going to leave you with a short demonstration of a document to help illustrate some of the things we've learned one more time.

I'm starting with the blank template, but I'm going to go a step further and delete the table in this template. So, I'm starting with something that is completely blank of any tables or objects.

Now I'm going to go to the table button and add in a table that has no formatting.

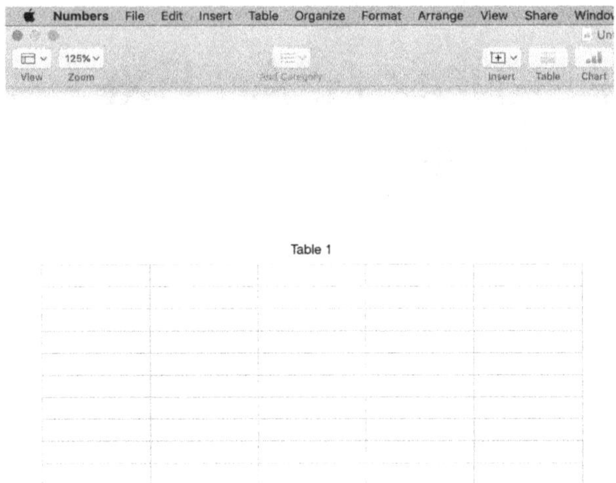

If you look at the example above, you'll notice some white space above the table. That's because I dragged it down a little. You can do the same by clicking and moving down the little circle in the corner of a selected table.

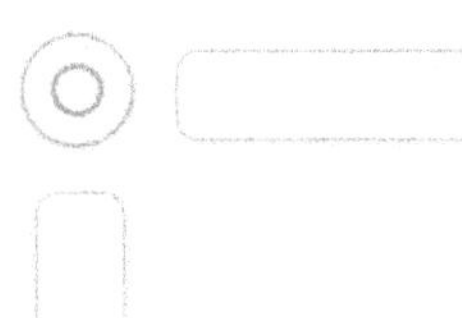

Next, I'm going to stick a logo on top of it. You can add your custom logo if you have an image already; for this example, I'm going to go to the Shapes icon and search for a barn.

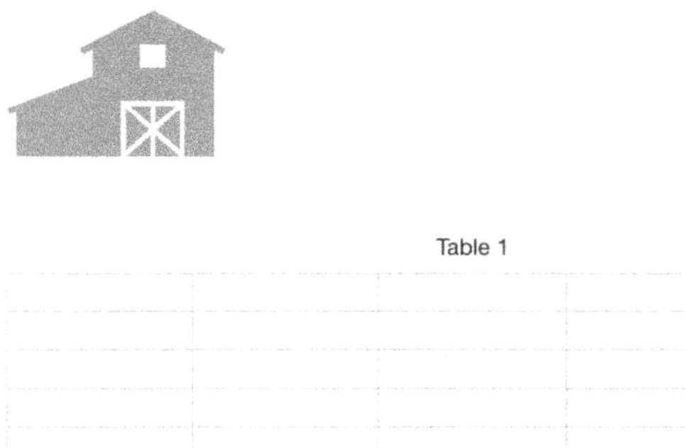

Now I need a title for my little project. I'm going to call it "My Barn Life." I'll move it to the top, and change the font size and color.

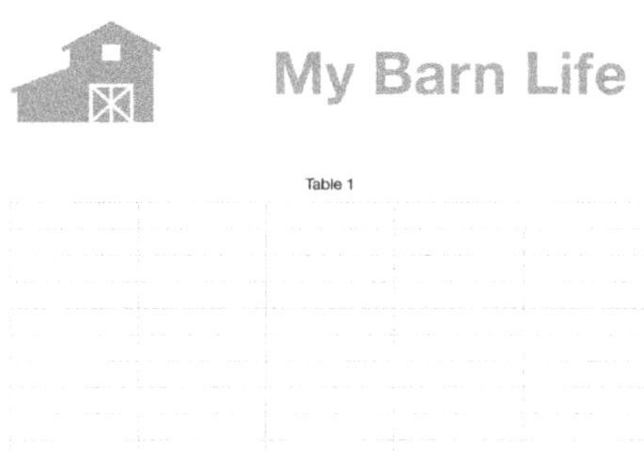

It's starting to come together. Next, I want to show an inventory of all the animals in my imaginary farm. I'm going to change the name of the table to "All My Animals" then create a list of the animal types and the number I have.

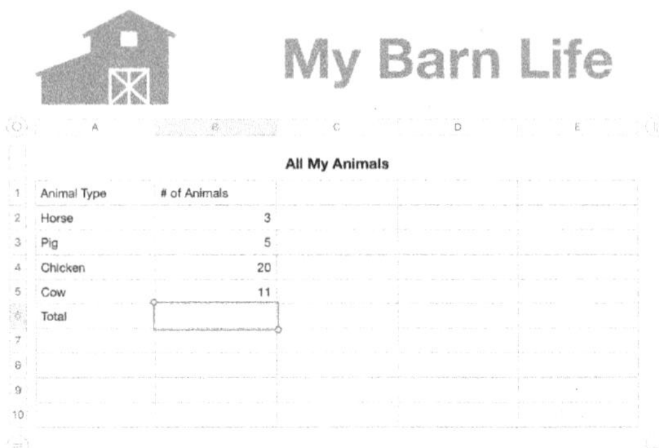

What's an inventory without counting the numbers? I'll do a very simple formula to add them all up by hitting the = key on the keyboard and then highlighting the cells with the number of animals.

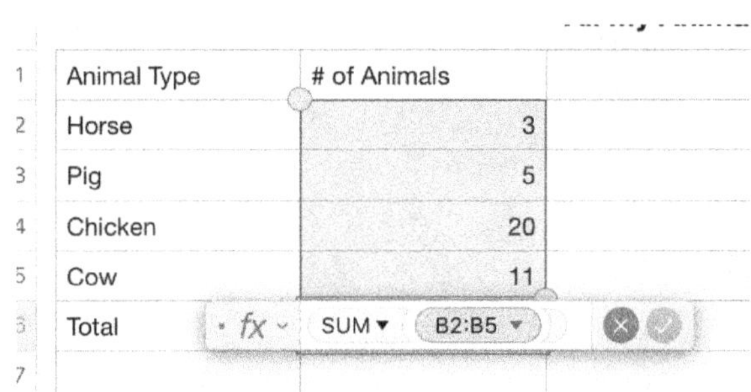

This is all helpful, but what would make it more helpful is if the table had more colors to make the rows pop out. I'm going to highlight cells that I want to change the color of, go to the Cell menu, then select a fill color.

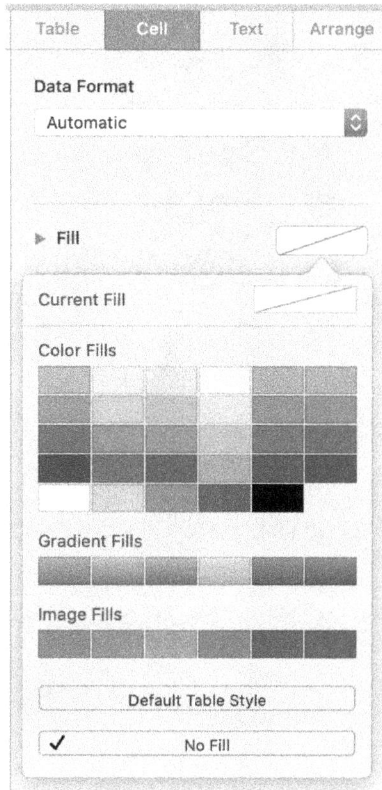

Now my table looks a little more eye-catching.

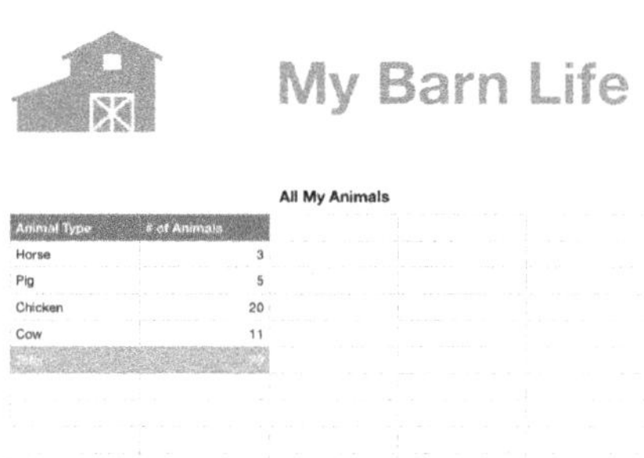

That's better, but there's no need for all of those extra cells. Let's delete them. Highlight the rows you want gone, then right click and select "Delete Selected Columns."

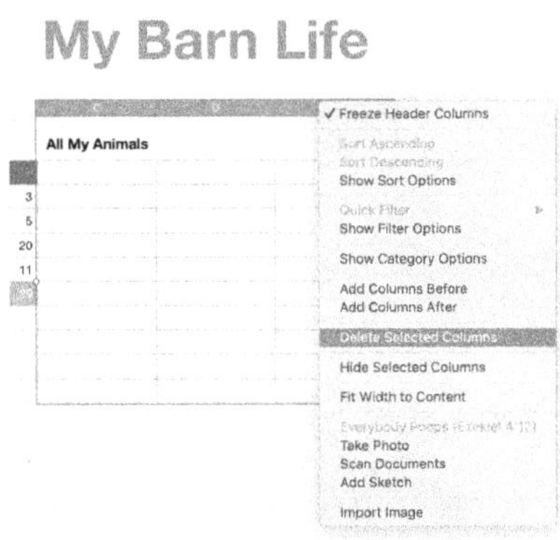

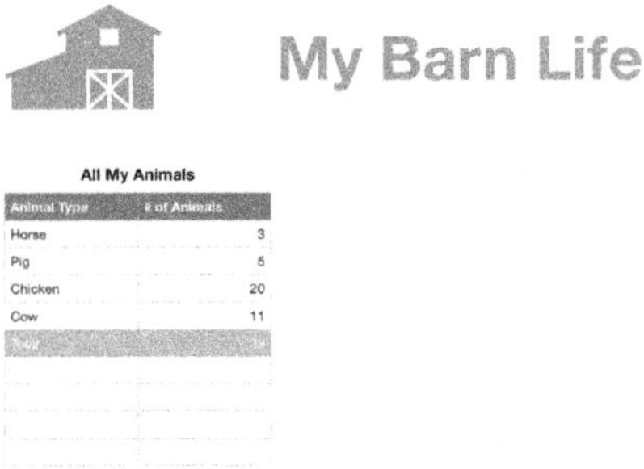

Now do the same for the bottom columns.

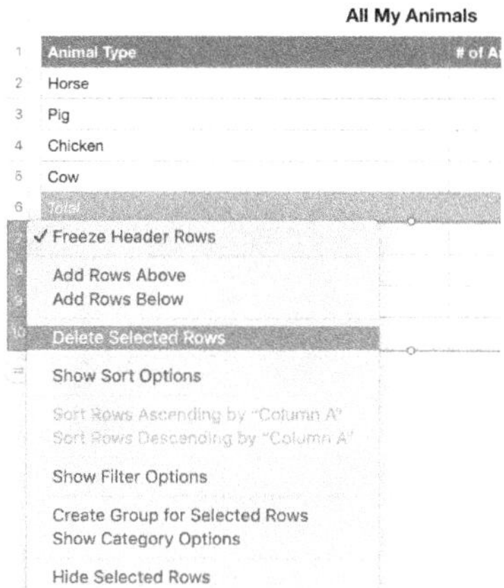

What list of barn animals would be complete without a graph?! Let's make a bar chart of all the animals so you can visually see what types make up the farm. Highlight the columns with numbers in them, then go to the chart button and select a pie chart.

You now have a lovely presentation of your life at the barn.

My Barn Life

All My Animals

Animal Type	# of Animals
Horse	3
Pig	5
Chicken	20
Cow	11
[illegible]	[illegible]

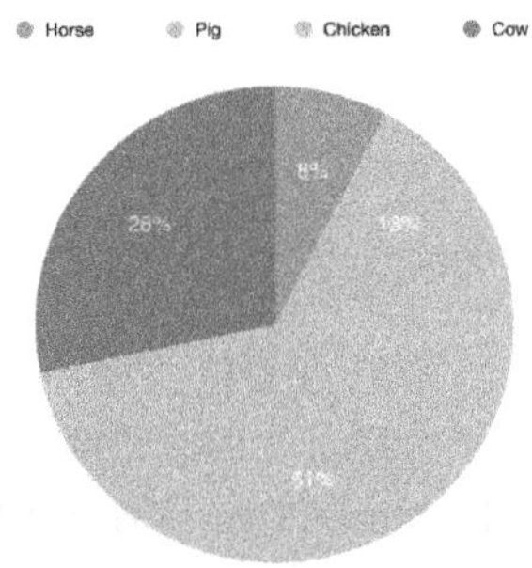

Appendix B: Keyboard Shortcuts

Action	**Shortcut**
Cmnd-N	Create new spreadsheet
Shft-Cmnd-N	Open Template Chooser
Cmnd-O	Open existing spreadsheet
Cmnd-S	Save
Shft-Cmnd-S	Save as
Cmnd-P	Print selected sheet
Cmnd-?	Open Numbers help
Cmnd-F	Find
Cmnd-G	Find next
Shft-Cmnd-G	Find previous
Cmnd->	Zoom in
Cmnd-<	Zoom out
Cmnd-Q	Quit Numbers
Cmnd-A	Select all text within selected object
Cmnd-T	Show Font panel
Cmnd-B	Make selected text bold
Cmnd-I	Make selected text italic
Cmnd-U	Underline selected text
Cmnd-X	Cut
Cmnd-C	Copy

Cmnd-V	Paste
Optn-Shft-Cmnd-V	Paste and match formatting of destination text
Optn-Space bar	Insert nonbreaking space
Shft-Return or Ctrl-Return	Insert line break (soft return)

About the Author

Scott La Counte is a librarian and writer. His first book, *Quiet, Please: Dispatches from a Public Librarian* (Da Capo 2008) was the editor's choice for the Chicago Tribune and a Discovery title for the Los Angeles Times; in 2011, he published the YA book The N00b Warriors, which became a #1 Amazon bestseller; his most recent book is *#OrganicJesus: Finding Your Way to an Unprocessed, GMO-Free Christianity* (Kregel 2016).

He has written dozens of best-selling how-to guides on tech products.

You can connect with him at ScottDouglas.org.

CPSIA information can be obtained
at www.ICGtesting.com
Printed in the USA
LVHW112044090321
680995LV00009BA/1642

9 781629 175140